"I see the Rise 2 Realize POWER Method not only as life changing but as shifting lineages, cultures, and social structures. In this time, there is a need for people who are grounded in something real, and the POWER Method is very real. It cuts to the core of what ails you, and does it fast. Transformation can be a beautiful and raw dance that dissolves what binds you and gently allows your powerful essence to emerge without a filter."

—Dionne D.

"I'm so grateful to have learned the Rise 2 Realize POWER Method when I was seeking help for my anger issues. The techniques in this method made me more conscious of my emotions. I'm amazed by the emotional balance and deeper understanding the Method has brought into my life."

—Namita N.

"I didn't like where I was in life. I was emotionally reacting to my husband, to my kids. I never knew how to prioritize my needs, so I always felt exhausted and drained. The Rise 2 Realize Method helped me get grounded right away. Using the tools made me shift the levels of happiness I was feeling not just for me, but for my family as well. I can now truly say that I haven't been happier in my life."

—Danielle G.

"I've been to countless counselors and therapists to try and deal with lingering issues. And yet . . . they kept lingering. Why? Because we keep repeating patterns over and over again. Applying the Rise 2 Realize POWER Method helped me identify my patterns that were hurting me. Over time, faster than I thought, I got to a place where I could clearly see, without fear, how I could move forward and take action for a better life."

—T.C.W.

"The Rise 2 Realize POWER Method helped me quickly identify and neutralize the things that were making me feel stressed and stuck. I was able to quickly learn to stay grounded and focused and feel more kindness and compassion for myself. As a result, I lost twenty pounds and now bring more energy and joy to my relationships."

—Amy S.

"Through the Rise 2 Realize POWER Method, I was able to find the guidance necessary to lead a more fulfilling life. For me, happiness is no longer an object of desire or a goal to achieve, it is a mindset and flow that has continued to permeate my career, my relationships, and every dimension of my life."

—Sean D.

"I was having real difficulty after the sudden passing of my younger sister. The Rise 2 Realize POWER Method guided me where others couldn't, using step-by-step inquiry and invitation to understand my path and triggers in a different way. The Method provided me comfort and healing and made me feel empowered."

—Lynnee J.

"The Rise 2 Realize POWER Method helped me understand my limiting thought patterns and behaviors. I now experience more fulfillment in my relationships. Life feels easier, brighter, and lighter."

—Hana R.

THE ART OF BECOMING

UNSTUCK

THE ART OF BECOMING
UNSTUCK

*your personalized journey through consciousness
in search of ultimate happiness*

ARDA OZDEMIR

Founder, Rise 2 Realize

RISE 2 REALIZE

The Art of Becoming Unstuck is for informational and
educational purposes only. The information contained in this
guidebook is based on the author's own experience and not
intended to diagnose, prescribe, treat, or cure any disease
or mental condition, or to replace the services of a licensed
therapist, mental health care provider, or physician.

Published by Rise 2 Realize, Palo Alto, CA
www.rise2realize.com

Edited and designed by Girl Friday Productions
www.girlfridayproductions.com

Design: Paul Barrett
Project management: Alexander Rigby
Image credits: cover photo © Shutterstock/koya979
(balloon), Shutterstock/jirapong (sky); Author
photo © Tati Scutelnic, tatiratita.com

ISBN (paperback): 978-0-9898104-1-8
ISBN (ebook): 978-0-9898104-2-5

First edition

Printed in the United States of America

Let the beauty we love be what we do.

There are hundreds of ways

to kneel and kiss the ground.

Out beyond ideas of wrongdoing

and rightdoing, there is a field.

I'll meet you there.

—Rumi

CONTENTS

FOREWORD

The book in your hands is much more than a practical life handbook—it is a mirror, a translation guide for your inner psyche, and most of all a reminder that you have everything you need *within you* to "unstuck" yourself and live the life you've wanted. In *The Art of Becoming Unstuck*, Arda Ozdemir adeptly coaches you through the mired waters of life using his POWER Method, offering freedom from life's triggers and repeating patterns. As much as "owning your emotions" is popular advice these days, there has been very little information on how to actually do that. Well, that information is here, for your eyes to read and mind to decipher and heart to embrace.

For many years, I have practiced as a Western physician with an integrative lens, widening the aperture of what it means to self-heal. What a relief it was when I met Arda, who is my perfect counterpart in this mission. Whereas I begin in the physical realm, Arda begins in the emotional, psychological, and spiritual realms, gently untangling the psyche through nonjudgmental inquiry and curiosity. I see our mutual patients transforming so beautifully over the course of their work with Arda. Once inner fears are heard and addressed, and patients are given tools for consciously working through their emotions, a sense of ease surrounds them. From my perspective, the results are clear—doctor visits for anxiety and stress-related health issues are virtually eliminated. But more important than that is a sense of confidence, meaning, vitality, and true happiness that I see emerging from patients who work with Arda's method. Now, with the publication of *The Art of Becoming Unstuck*, the wider community has access to Arda's coaching. This very practical guidebook is written as if he were sitting at your side, helping you to learn about your own inner workings with the same gentleness and encouragement that he displays while advising in his own practice.

Arda is the consummate self-empowerment coach, helping each individual to find answers using life itself (and one's reactions to it) as the guide. His POWER Method for demystifying and managing emotions is effective for anyone curious enough to go deeper into their own limiting patterns of thought in order to process and neutralize them. Thus, the attainment of ultimate gratitude, happiness, and love is taught in a style reminiscent of the ancient mystics. Your *reaction* to the world is a personalized guide, and it *lights the way toward* everything you are meant to learn and know.

I caution the reader that *The Art of Becoming Unstuck* is not an easy path. Prepare to get raw, vulnerable, and very real with yourself. The more you do, the more you will transform. This is the equivalent of standing in front of a mirror, naked. With the POWER Method, you will reveal your unmasked soul, spirit, and ego. You will be guided to push beyond the resistance, the hurt, and the defensiveness that you might think protects you, in order to release these emotions and be free once and for all. What awaits on the other side is immense healing, authenticity, and joy. I hope you find the gifts from this work as priceless as I have and wish you well in the journey!

Gina Serraiocco, MD
Fellow Seeker
Board-certified Internal Medicine
Board-certified Integrative Medicine

INTRODUCTION

HOW THE POWER METHOD CAME TO LIFE

It was the summer of 1973, and I was at a summer camp on the west coast of Turkey. During one of the after-dinner party nights for the kids, I got up and walked across the stage to ask a girl whom I had a crush on to dance with me. She said yes. I was so excited that I was smiling from ear to ear. We made our way to the dance floor and started swinging to the music. We were moving all over the dance floor. I was on cloud nine. And then, for a split second, I saw my friends, standing on the side. They were laughing at me, making fun of me, mocking me for dancing so joyfully and being carefree. I was just six years old when I learned that I couldn't be me.

Around noontime on a beautiful spring day, when I was nine years old, my class was about to go to the schoolyard to play games and throw the ball, to have fun and enjoy the warm weather. Out of excitement, I started singing "Neşeli Gençleriz," or "We Are Happy Youngsters," which was the popular song of the day. All of a sudden, I heard my teacher across the classroom shouting at me, warning me not to sing such songs out loud. I didn't know what *such songs* meant, but once again I learned that I couldn't be me.

When I was twelve, it was all about grades. The persistent message I heard was *study hard to get into high school.* In a developing country like Turkey, success depended on grades and what school you went to. It was a very competitive environment. There was no such thing as playing, exploring, or expressing yourself. Life was all about studying books, attending exam-preparation courses, and shuttling between school and home. Life didn't exist outside of these parameters. It was not how you experienced life that mattered, but what you could accomplish in life. I once again learned that I couldn't be me.

During the spring of 1991, I developed excruciating headaches. I had one month left before I'd graduate from college, and it was time to choose my career. But even after having been locked in schools for eighteen years, I still didn't know where to go. I didn't know what I wanted. I didn't know who I was. How was I supposed to choose a career for my life without knowing who I was? Although I'd be graduating with a degree in business management, I was still struggling to choose my right path. Should I pursue product marketing? Public accounting? Corporate finance? Investment banking? Advertising? I was twenty-four years old and had learned that I couldn't be me, for I didn't know who I was.

Still later in life, I began to think that everything has a preconceived purpose, with predetermined goals and regulations we are all expected to comply with. We go to high school to be admitted to college. We go to college to find a career. We find a career to start a job. We start a job to save money. We save money to retire one day. We retire one day to enjoy life. We enjoy life to die without regret. Everything has a goal. We constantly comply with these goals, norms, and regulations, which are set by society, our parents, our teachers, our environment, and our friends. We follow this guidance to a *T,* hoping to find happiness. But life feels heavier and heavier each day that we conform to external expectations.

By the time I was thirty-three years old, life under the obligations and expectations that others had put upon me had begun to feel terribly heavy. I felt trapped as a certified public accountant, grinding through endless hours of auditing financial records of public companies without any sense of personal purpose or connection to what I was doing. And yet I had nowhere to go but work. The nightmare continued.

And then, when I was thirty-nine and had worked my way up the corporate finance ladder in Silicon Valley, I started to get sick. Physically exhausted and sleep-deprived, I began suffering from sinus infections every month. Every other month, the infections turned into bronchitis. Every three months, my bronchitis turned into pneumonia. Like clockwork. And following the pneumonia, with all the coughing and sleepless nights, laryngitis would often come along, taking my voice away for a week or so. This went on for two years.

A dark, burned log settled within my heart as deep anxiety and depression coursed through my body. I felt confused about life. Why was I in this situation? What else could I have done? I had checked off every item on life's checklist—good grades, a good job, and so on—yet everything I thought would bring me happiness had become a source of disappointment and stress. The more I thought about it, the more I began to realize that these so-called accomplishments were just pieces of paper that built my house of cards. They weren't reality, and now they were falling apart. I felt betrayed by life. I felt lost. I felt stuck.

I had no choice but to start my search for a New Life, a better life. I could have turned to prescription drugs to numb my depression, anxiety, and sadness, but instead I decided to figure out who I was and how I had gotten myself into this position, this low state. To find my Self and determine why I'd been living my life this way. From my first step, I realized I was making a serious decision that would affect my entire life going forward. The possibility of change was very scary in the beginning. I knew I had to leave my comfort zone. I knew I needed to challenge the security I'd built over the years. I knew it was going to be difficult to face my Self and analyze some of my life experiences in a way I had not done before.

During these times of self-reflection and search for meaning, my partner at the time, Elif Kuvvetli, introduced me to an amazing intuitive healer, Naz McSweeney, who opened the doors to the meaning of my life and helped me begin to understand who I really was. While I was working with her, I randomly ran into my old college friend from Turkey, Nil Demirçubuk, on the streets of San Francisco. Out of the blue, she helped me heal my sinus infections by introducing me to Reiki, a Japanese healing art. Later, she also suggested that Elif and I visit Master Zhao, a Qigong master, for a few other health concerns I was having. He then became my teacher and introduced me to the ancient meditation practices of Qigong and the energetic pathways of meridians that form the foundation of traditional Chinese medicine.

It felt like I was being guided to work on my health issues and find the meaning of my life. All of these healing methods helped me so much with my sinus infections that I decided to learn more about them. As I practiced them and witnessed the incredible health benefits of these techniques, I wanted to share them with others. Keep in mind that I was still immersed in the corporate world, and I was still skeptical. At the same time, I was experiencing such tangible, visible, and palpable benefits to my mental, emotional, and physical state of being that it was hard to refute these ancient healing modalities and meditation techniques.

The word got out. I slowly started developing a private practice and bringing in my first clients, hoping to share what I knew and be of service to others. Everything started to shift from that point on. I garnered so much more fulfillment from meeting just a few clients a week than I had from my role as a high-tech VP of finance. That's when I realized that this was undeniably my calling, and I decided to leave everything else behind.

A few years after I opened my practice, a Mikkyo Buddhist Zen monk, Koraku-san, came to my office and asked me if I'd be interested in becoming a monk. I was profoundly surprised and grateful, and I immediately said yes and started my training. Meanwhile, I was also studying hypnotherapy. Since my childhood, the study of the human psyche had always fascinated me, yet I'd never found time to learn more about how the subconscious mind works.

By now I was able to incorporate all of the disciplines and modalities I had been studying into my sessions. I admittedly was a bit surprised—but also overjoyed—to discover that my clients were experiencing miraculous transformations—not in years, not in months, but in weeks. In February 2014, I published *The Seeker's Manual* for current and future clients, to summarize what I'd learned so far and to offer a roadmap of a typical seven-phase personal growth journey. I also developed a corresponding workshop called *Journey Within*. The workshop participants responded very positively, confirming they indeed experienced a transformational shift in just three to four weeks. Yet I sensed there was still something missing, maybe an element or a technique that would bring everything together for a deeper, quicker, even more profound personal and spiritual transformation.

The second wave of my exploration for deeper truth about Self and Life started in August 2016. Around this time, an intuitive astrologer I was working with, Jo'ann Ruhl, mentioned

Nine Gates Mystery School, a program taught by interspiritual teachers from Celtic, African, Native American, Hindu, Buddhist, and other traditions that focuses on the embodiment of the inner self. The timing was perfect for me, and I enrolled right before the semester started.

About a year after Nine Gates, Meenakshi Singh, one of my former colleagues from the corporate world, randomly called me—ten years after our last conversation—to invite me to a reception to meet Dr. Richard Miller, who is well known for his teachings about ancient yogic traditions from Northern India known as Yoga Nidra. While I was attending one of his Yoga Nidra retreats, Dr. Miller mentioned George Gurdjieff, a Russian philosopher and mystic from the early 1900s who founded the Fourth Way, a transformational perspective on Eastern spiritual thinking and philosophy. A few months later, a friend of a client of mine invited me to join the San Francisco Gurdjieff Society, where I attended weekly group-study meetings for a few years, learning about Gurdjieff and his remarkable perspective on human behavior.

Until this time, I'd been testing and experimenting with techniques I'd learned in every school, course, seminar, and lecture I attended. As soon as I experienced the transformative effects of a technique in my own life, I immediately incorporated it into my sessions to see how my clients would respond. After many iterations and trials and errors, like a scientist testing his hypothesis, I concluded that the missing element from all these methods and techniques was the body. I needed to incorporate the physical body into the transformational journey. As I reviewed all that I'd learned since I left the corporate world, the word magically appeared in front of me:

POWER. Pause. Observe. Welcome. Earth. Respond.

PAUSE was inspired by Gurdjieff's teachings and the practice of stopping and taking note of what's happening around us.

OBSERVE was inspired by the Mikkyo Zen Buddhist practice of active meditation that involves observing our thoughts as they appear in the mind.

WELCOME was inspired by Yoga Nidra and Dr. Miller's gentle guidance to acknowledge whatever arises in the body.

EARTH was inspired by my Qigong teacher, Master Zhao, who pointed toward the feet to ground and center our energies before any activity.

And RESPOND refers to how individuals who become self-aware receive life and its challenges and connect with their inner power to consciously discern their actions as responses rather than reactions.

Now, after a decade of research, experimentation, and contemplation, the formula is ready to be shared with everyone interested in rising above their ordinary life, above the matrix toward Ultimate Happiness—a New Life, a high life, a life full of love, joy, abundance, fulfillment, meaning, and purpose. *The Art of Becoming Unstuck* was born from the personal transformation journey I was guided to take, and I now invite you to embark on your own incredibly rewarding self-discovery journey.

This book is intended to be a guide on your path to self-realization. I hope all the wisdom, the teachings, and the guidance passed on to me will become a source of empowerment for you and propel you toward your Truth. If you are called to embark on this blessed journey, many rewards and gifts await you, including the discovery of your Real Self and the higher life you are meant to live. As in all guidebooks, this is a starting point, not the end of the journey. If you choose to continue further and dig deeper into the inner workings of your psyche, I'd highly recommend you attend a "Life Skills 101: The Art of Becoming Unstuck" group workshop, held every six months. You can also download the Rise 2 Realize meditation app, which will help you with the emotional cleansing and mastery we explore in this book. You can visit www.Rise2Realize.com to find the dates of upcoming workshops and links to the meditation app.

You can master art through practice. Throughout this guidebook, you'll encounter a variety of life skills assignments that I encourage you to treat as if they were breadcrumbs intentionally leading you to a special place. You'll also discover a collection of life laws: truths about how to navigate life to find Ultimate Happiness. In a sense, each assignment guides you to turn inward, while each law invites you to look outward to examine life.

As you move through *The Art of Becoming Unstuck*, try to incorporate the life skills assignments into your daily practices and contemplate life laws with a meditative and observant mind. Notice the shifts in your consciousness. Witness the intricate workings of your subconscious mind as they are revealed. Take note when some of life's mysteries become unlocked. And celebrate as the doors to your Real Self are opened. It is in your life experiences, and not in my words, where you'll find the true evidence of your transformation and experience glimpses of Ultimate Happiness.

CHAPTER ONE

IDENTIFYING WHAT MAKES YOU FEEL STUCK

Once upon a time in Japan, two seasoned monks, Tanzan and Ekido, were traveling together on foot when a heavy rain started to fall. Shortly thereafter, they came to an intersection where they saw a young, beautiful girl in a silk kimono who was unable to cross the muddy road.

With no hesitation, Tanzan jumped ahead, lifted her up, and carried her over the mud to the other side of the road.

Even though Ekido was in complete shock afterward, he couldn't voice his distaste until late that night, when both were resting at the lodging temple. "Don't you remember our oath not to go near women?" he said irritably. "Especially young women like the one we saw today. Why did you do that?"

Tanzan slowly turned his eyes to Ekido and replied, "I left the girl at the intersection. Why are you still carrying her?"

How did Tanzan move on so quickly, without being bothered by either Ekido's judgment or his own violation of a sacred rule, while Ekido got all jumbled up in his mind and couldn't let go of what he saw? Is it because, as an older monk, Tanzan is more trained in controlling his thoughts and reactions than Ekido? Does he have more willpower? Has he done more meditations, recited more mantras?

Before we answer these questions, let's remember not to be too critical of Ekido. You and I are not that different from him. We all naturally react to people or situations that don't align with our values or belief systems. It's part of life to judge and react to others' negative attitudes, bad behaviors, annoying personalities, condescending actions, or critical words. To that extent, consider some of the following life situations and reflect on what happens to you when others:

- criticize you and put you down,
- don't pay attention to you,
- don't appreciate what you do for them,
- don't call you as often as you wish,
- don't value your work or input,
- don't follow your instructions,
- demand too much of your time,
- interrupt you,
- make you feel not good enough,
- gossip about you behind your back,
- don't share or accept your values,
- don't invite you to their parties,
- don't listen to you while you're talking, or
- don't really care what you're trying to say.

So, what do you do when these things happen to you?

Most probably, you react emotionally to these people and situations! And nothing's wrong with your emotional reactions. But for exploration purposes, let's review their consequences.

REASONS BEHIND FEELING STUCK

Even though an emotional reaction is neither good nor bad, at the end of the day, it is an energy drainer, leaving you feeling depleted afterward. Worse yet, these situations often lead to conflict with others, leaving you even more exhausted and drained. Negative thoughts rush into your head and occupy your mind for hours, for days—maybe even for weeks. Sometimes you can't easily shake them off or let them go, as Tanzan could, and with little energy left for anyone or anything else, you feel stuck and lost, blaming the situation and other people for your unhappiness.

Upon closer look, though, these situations and people seem to repeat in your life. When the cycle of emotional reactions and depletion of your energy continues, you start to feel more stuck, lost, and confused.

For example, if you're in the dating scene, you might have found that you've been attracting similar people over and over again—people who are possessive, or emotionally unavailable, or abusive, or noncommittal, or unfaithful. Or they're the people who often put you down. Or they ghost you after a few dates without any apparent reason. Or they're self-absorbed and not thoughtful enough to care about you or get to know you. Any of these dating partners could understandably make you feel unhappy, lonely, unattractive, not valued—maybe not even dateable. And yet, you keep attracting them into your life, and you feel stuck.

How about at home with your significant other? Have you had enough of those petty arguments about how to load the dishwasher, or how to organize the refrigerator, or how to make a list for groceries? Have you found yourself complaining about constantly being talked over, or being put down for talking nonsense? Has your partner stopped wanting to go on a date night as a couple, or even make eye contact when talking with you? What happened to the physical intimacy or emotional closeness that you both once had? When repeated, these situations can certainly make you feel unhappy, unworthy, invisible, not good enough. And yet, you keep attracting these arguments and situations into your life, and you feel stuck.

In your career, you might have a tendency to choose dead-end jobs, or positions with bad bosses in which, no matter what you do, you never receive credit for your work. Or maybe you've never had a fulfilling job. Or your colleagues never recognize your ideas as valid. Or you were repeatedly skipped over when it came time for promotions. Whatever jobs you hold can make you feel unhappy, unrecognized, unvalued, not good enough; you might even feel like a failure. And yet, you keep attracting these unfulfilling jobs and unappreciative bosses, and you feel stuck.

On the money front, you might have made bad financial decisions over and over again. Maybe you still have growing credit card debt that you always promise to pay off, but you can't quite get around to it because, whenever you go out, you always end up spending too much money. Or no matter what you do for a living, you don't seem to earn quite enough money or land quite the right salary or generally attract enough good fortune. When you always seem to be in debt or otherwise out of control financially, you feel unhappy, unworthy, like a failure yet again, and certainly not successful. And yet, you keep attracting financial misfortune, and you feel stuck.

In your personal life, you might have made a lot of promises to yourself: don't watch the news, stop binging on junk food and sweets, go to bed earlier, quit smoking, stop working so many long hours for your job, eliminate video games from your life, cut back on the wine consumption, get off social media, refrain from ever touching another card at the blackjack table, stop watching porn every night, get to meetings on time, or stop yelling at your kids when you're angry. And every time you do—every time you fail to create a better life for yourself—you wind up feeling unhappy and not good enough. You doubt yourself and your self-worth. And yet, you keep breaking your self-promises over and over again, and you feel stuck.

I've certainly had my fair share of these situations in my life. For a long time, I kept attracting emotionally unavailable people, whether as dating partners or as friends, and I felt lonely and lost as I worried whether I'd ever be able to find someone to deeply connect with. I changed jobs five times in seven years due to the attitudes I encountered in my bosses and colleagues, unable to find a corporate culture that fit my values. Throughout most of my life, since early childhood, I had a sense of not being seen, heard, or recognized by others, whether I was in a family gathering, in a corporate meeting, or hanging out with my friends. I often felt confused and vulnerable, believing I didn't belong anywhere. I felt stuck and, at times, even trapped.

What is going on here? Who are these people and what are these situations that keep repeating in life, making you, me, and everyone else feel stuck?

They are called limiting life patterns—and they are why we all feel confused, lost, trapped, and stuck.

Let's take a closer look at them.

LIMITING LIFE PATTERNS

As you can see from the above examples, it is not one person or situation that makes you feel stuck. It is a pattern that appears periodically in your life. Different people and situations provoke the same emotions, yield the same outcomes, and bring up the same feelings. Life runs through these patterns, which are woven into your relationships with everyone and everything, even with yourself, and you are constantly subject to them, which can deprive you of happiness until you learn to break free. These patterns are why you feel like you're on a hamster wheel, with no exit door in sight. You keep running and running, sometimes to the point of feeling nauseated, even though you think you're in pursuit of happiness. Wouldn't it make more sense to find a way to rise above these limiting life patterns, to free yourself from the negative effects of those people and things that bring you down?

Before we dive deep into techniques on how to rise above limiting life patterns, let's explore why you create these patterns in the first place. Bruce Lipton, renowned cell biologist and author of *The Biology of Belief: Unleashing the Power of Consciousness, Matter and Miracles*, says most of your actions are controlled by your subconscious internal programming and are designed for your survival. In other words, none of your life decisions are made to help you "live life."

Instead, you and your subconscious create a comfort zone beneath the overarching goal of survival, hedging life's uncertainties. You surround yourself with people and accumulate things so that you feel safe and happy. You create checklists for life, ticking off every box on the list: where to go to college, what career to choose, what partner to marry, where to live, what house to buy, what car to drive, what kind of friends to have, where to go for vacation.

But even when things don't go according to plan, you keep repeating the same behaviors because that's what your comfort zone calls for. With every expectation and decision that leads to disappointment, you return to your checklist and tick off the boxes again without changing the design or features of the comfort zone you've created for your survival and safety in the first place. You tighten up your choices and close down even more, believing this is what you must do to make it in life. But what happens is that, ultimately, your comfort zone becomes suffocating. You try to run away from those people who make you unhappy. You try to escape from those situations that challenge your security. Yet you keep going in the same circles and end up running into them, or variations of them, over and over. One letdown after another, you become more stuck, lost, and confused.

You are not alone. Everyone is subject to these limiting life patterns. I remember one that I experienced when I was in the corporate world, first as a corporate controller and later as a vice president of finance. I changed my job five times over a seven-year period pretty much for the same reason: lack of recognition from my boss and my colleagues. For example, at one of the companies, I once chose and implemented a new revenue accounting process to streamline and enhance our financial reporting systems, but although everyone raved about how much better it was than our old, obsolete system, no one thanked me or praised me for a job well done. The success of that project, which had consumed a major part of my work year and cost me my health, warranted neither a mention in my annual performance review nor a pat on the back. I left that job for another at a new company, where I yet again faced similar treatment by my boss and peers.

Years passed, and I couldn't figure out how to break this vicious cycle—until my last corporate gig, where I stayed for four and a half years. Surprisingly, at this job I was still exposed to some of the lack of recognition that I faced in my earlier jobs. However, this time, I responded to them differently because I had started practicing the techniques that I describe in this book. First I became aware of my limiting life patterns. Then I understood why I was falling into them. And, lastly, I applied the tools to break free from them. As a result, I was able to stay in this final corporate position longer than I had stayed in previous workplaces, since I'd managed to rise above my old triggers.

Let me tell you about another limiting life pattern of mine. Since my childhood, I have felt a little different from others— the way I do things or the way I think about things. This difference has attracted mockery and dismissal from others. Wherever I went, whomever I met, I felt a *putting down* attitude from them. This limiting life pattern might have started early in my childhood when my dad was unable to value me as a person or understand who I was or where I was coming from, no matter what the topic was. For example, one day we were about to go on a vacation. I was struggling to fit our luggage into the trunk of our car, and he laughed at my failed attempts, blaming my different way of thinking on the fact that I had a caesarean birth. Decades after that incident, I was learning to sail. It was supposed to be fun, yet I brought my pattern into that experience as well. The instructor made fun of me struggling at the helm, even though I noticed the other two students made similar, even worse mistakes than me and yet somehow were spared the instructor's sarcastic comments. These are just two instances of many spread over the decades. Since I did not know how to get out of these situations and find my way to personal and emotional freedom, I kept attracting them into my life.

There is no end to limiting life patterns in one's life. Another pattern involved my former partner. After we moved together to Sydney, Australia, from Istanbul, Turkey, we wound up having the exact same arguments and attitudes that I used to get exposed to back home with my parents. I was shocked. I wondered how this could possibly be happening. One of the arguments was about having a messy desk. Another was about leaving dishes in the sink overnight. My partner also kept criticizing me for not picking up my stuff around the house even though we had a meticulous home. We had moved 8,111 miles away from my parents, and yet I was still subject to the same criticism. I wondered how she could say the same things to me, in that same critical and judgmental tone that my parents used to call me out on my shortcomings or failures to meet their expectations. I was twenty-seven then, too young to recognize that limiting life patterns had already begun to shape my future, and there would be no way to escape them until I was in my late forties.

Even though my personal experiences with these limiting life patterns were emotionally painful and made me feel worthless, not recognized, trapped, stuck, lost, dismissed, or misplaced, I now know that they've been inviting me to open my eyes, a little bit at a time, to eventually see the System of Life. When I started to see them as open invitations for personal discovery, the mysteries of life began to reveal themselves and allow me to stop blaming others, for I understood that they had no ill will or conscious intention to hurt me. On the contrary, these painful experiences paved the way for me to learn tools and techniques to rise above them and prompted me to search for deeper personal and spiritual growth, to finally realize the Ultimate Happiness I was destined for.

Law of Life #1:
Rise above limiting life patterns to realize Ultimate Happiness.

Limiting life patterns are the fabric of life, the structure within the matrix, the system designed to push our buttons and tighten our comfort zones so that we must search for answers. All patterns force us to go inward to find our inner strength. In other words, they're meant to serve as guidance on how we can take our lives back from the governance, the stronghold, and the influence of our subconscious internal programming.

We must consciously work to take our lives into our hands so we can rise above our limiting life patterns, above the matrix, and respond to others, and to life, in a completely different way that preserves our mental and emotional balance. Only from that state of balance can life open doors for you, for me, and for everyone, leading us together to new possibilities and positive experiences in life, where we can all find more love, joy, abundance, fulfillment, and meaning, which is the Ultimate Happiness that we all deserve as our highest potential in life.

LEVELS OF CONSCIOUSNESS

How do we achieve mental and emotional balance to become unstuck and realize Ultimate Happiness?

By overcoming subconscious internal programming.

Let's walk through a logical deduction. What really makes us feel stuck is that we keep emotionally and defensively reacting to our limiting life patterns, hoping that they'll disappear. Yet nothing changes, as we keep finding ourselves back in these patterns over and over again. As a result, we can conclude that our emotional reactions and defensive actions, which are an integral part of our survival mechanisms, are not effective tools to break free from our limiting life patterns. Since our subconscious internal programming creates these survival mechanisms, if we want to rise above our patterns and become unstuck, we need to rise in consciousness and overcome that programming.

Then the next logical question is, how do we rise in consciousness?

By definition, consciousness means awareness of the mind itself and of the external world. We can argue that when we are controlled by our subconscious internal programming, our mind is furthest away from an awareness of the internal and external world, and it is therefore unable to recognize, understand, and break free from the limiting life patterns that are part of our subconscious survival mechanisms. We must become aware of these patterns and understand why they exist by using a different level of consciousness, one which is higher than our subconscious.

Well, what are these different levels of consciousness that we need to rise through?

Let's examine the levels of consciousness to provide a reference point for exploring questions about our lives, particularly why we attract certain life experiences, why we do things the way we do, why we feel stuck and trapped within our limiting life patterns, why we live under the weight of these survival mechanisms, and why we are where we are in our lives. This will help us identify ways to reach levels of consciousness that will naturally guide us toward our highest potential, Ultimate Happiness.

We'll start by assessing what your current level of consciousness might be.

The first level is the *subconscious*. This is where you live in survival mode, subject to the fight-or-flight operating system. Here, your life is controlled by subconscious internal programming and you operate within your limiting life patterns, which makes you feel stuck and creates confusion and suffering in your life. At this consciousness level, you tend to be sensitive and take things personally, and as a result, you are almost always in an emotionally reactive state, defensive against people and situations. Life seems to be heavy, turbulent, chaotic, and full of patterns that are intense and repeat frequently.

Living at this level can feel like driving on a country road with lots of potholes. Not a pleasant ride. Your days are filled with mental and emotional hardship, suffering, and the sense of being in a permanently reactive state. This level can be described as *chasing happiness*, to denote the pursuit of happiness that is supposedly out there, outside of your Self, but clearly beyond your present reach.

The second level of consciousness is called the *self-conscious*. At this level, you are more aware of your subconscious internal programming and can observe it in the context of your limiting life patterns. Through a practice of observation, which we'll discuss in greater detail in future chapters, you can slow down your survival instincts and shift power from your subconscious to your self-conscious. You can gain deeper insights into why you do the things you do, and why you do them in a particular way. You can even acknowledge the underlying causes of your emotional reactions and their impact on your life's decisions.

This watchful state creates a sense of more breathing space and an ability to initiate discernment and discrimination in your actions. At this consciousness level, you become more and more aware of your actions and the consequences of your reactions, learning the cause and effect of your life's decisions. Slowly, you take more control of your life and make mindful and intentional choices that yield happier outcomes. You respond to people and situations from a more mentally and emotionally balanced state, and when you do, you realize you have more energy to cope with the inevitable challenges that come your way.

You enjoy life overall. You have more time and energy for your hobbies and creative outlets. You are more aware of things that you haven't noticed before. You experience synchronicities more frequently. You establish deeper connections with others. You discover greater opportunities for authentic self-expression to showcase your Self in all areas of your life. You live more from your heart as your limiting life patterns begin to fade, gradually losing their momentum and intensity. When you first arrive at this level, you might experience them once a month, then every three months, and then every six months or so. Your quality of life increases substantially. Living at this level feels like driving on a well-paved street in a metropolitan city with clear lanes, nicely groomed trees on each side, and a smooth flow of traffic. This level can be called *choosing happiness*, as the decision to be happy is now in your hands.

The third level of consciousness is the *high-conscious*. At this level, you are no longer in survival mode. You are fully in charge of your life. You live in a complete flow state where your mind and your heart work together for the right action. You constantly operate from a higher integrity point that empowers you to take actions completely aligned with your essence and the true nature of your Self. You feel more authentic and more in your own element, and you see many opportunities for growth in any given moment. Life is full of possibilities, full of higher potential.

When you live at this level, you feel like you're driving on a German autobahn. Life is now a smooth ride with no bumps. You have a driving experience in which you connect with the road and surroundings, get in the zone, and advance along your journey without interruption. You start to experience a sense of deep commitment, a genuine trust in life, and a confidence that everything will fall into place. You rarely take things personally, and you live completely according to your own values, full of energy and deep feelings of love, joy, and fulfillment. This level can be described as Ultimate Happiness.

Have you ever felt this kind of flow state?

Imagine you are looking for a parking spot in the middle of lunch rush hour at a busy shopping mall. You drive in and feel a strange urge to turn left. You do so, but wonder why. All of a sudden, you see another car's reverse lights illuminating. You stop. You turn your blinker on. You gently smile and think, *Of course!* The car pulls out. There's your parking spot.

This kind of high-conscious flow feels like smooth sailing, and it can happen anywhere. At work, for example, you might

suddenly get in the zone during a project and everything falls
into place: you have a sharp focus, you're more efficient, and
you complete your tasks effortlessly. At home, you might find
laughter and joy, everyone getting along with each other. You
bond with your partner and your kids, and you get things done
without arguments or conflicts.

Achieving this ideal flow state, especially when you're feeling stuck within your limiting life patterns, can sound like a
daunting task. It is actually quite doable, however, because the
levels aren't finite stops along your journey. Rather, they represent a continuum of consciousness, and one of our goals is
to learn to shift our position along this continuum. Imagine, if
you will, that each of the three consciousness levels is assigned
a numerical range; for example, the subconscious might be
assigned a range of 1 through 55, the self-conscious level might
be 56 through 85, and the high-conscious level would be 86
through 100. Now ask yourself this: What if life is config-
ured to meet you at exactly your consciousness level? In other
words, what if you're at level 35, and the frequency, intensity,
and quality of your limiting life patterns reflects exactly level
35? What if you increase your consciousness level to 65? Can
you imagine what kind of life you'll be living at that level?

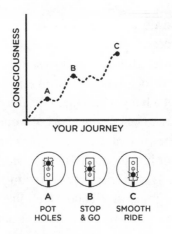

What this means is that, at lower consciousness levels, you're more dependent on your survival mechanisms. Living at higher consciousness levels means being less subject to those unhealthy, limiting life patterns, giving you more space, energy, freedom, flow, and green lights to experience joy, love, and fulfillment. If all of this is part of a design, part of a system, then what can you possibly do to rise out of that lower, confining level of your subconscious and progress toward 100, toward your highest potential, where you can live at the level of Ultimate Happiness?

DECODING THE SUBCONSCIOUS

Before we go deeper into how to rise, we need to spend a little more time understanding our present level of consciousness. And to do that, we're going to start at the lowest level, the subconscious, and look at how to decode subconscious internal programming.

How can you decode, or decipher, what's in your subconscious? By understanding why you are where you are—and there is certainly a reason.

Imagine a hot air balloon, an aircraft consisting of a single-layer fabric bag, called the envelope, that is tied to a basket or gondola, which is surrounded by sandbags. The gas tank underneath the mouth of this envelope heats the air trapped inside it, making the hot air balloon rise, since the air inside the envelope has a lower density than the colder air outside of it. When the pilot wants to bring the hot air balloon down, he simply stops the fire from heating the air, allowing the temperature inside the balloon to drop and equalize with the surrounding outside air. Then the weight of the sandbags ultimately brings the balloon back to the ground. Of course, when the gas tank is empty, the same thing happens: the air inside the balloon cools and the sandbags bring the balloon down.

Now, what if the mechanical up-and-down ride of the hot air balloon is a perfect replica of how life flows? What if the altitudes you travel to in this hot air balloon correspond to the levels of your consciousness and your happiness? What if, all your life, you've tried to reach higher altitudes and smooth sailing, but you keep spending too much energy at lower levels, emptying your fuel tank and having to descend over and over again? What if, having depleted the energy in your tank, you've reluctantly had to watch your sandbags pull you down, back to where you were, back to tumultuous lower altitudes, back to your tight comfort zone and survival mechanisms, back to challenging situations, difficult people and negative thoughts?

In that case, wouldn't it make more sense to get rid of your sandbags first so that you require less effort, less fire, less energy to rise above lower altitudes toward calmer, smoother, higher elevations? But how can you release your sandbags? You can only release them by thoroughly decoding and understanding the inner workings of your subconscious internal programming—basically, the operating system of the survival mechanism that created your sandbags in the first place.

What *is* a sandbag, then?

Sandbags represent those aspects of your personality and psyche that you don't want to admit you have. They are the parts of your subconscious internal programming that you never dare to face. They are the vulnerabilities that pull you down to lower altitudes and determine the level of your consciousness, directly affecting the intensity and frequency of your limiting life patterns. As we've already discussed, the lower your consciousness level, the more intense and frequent your limiting life patterns will be; conversely, the higher your level, the less intense and frequent.

In order to heal your vulnerability and release your sandbags, you need to be able to identify them. And you do this by noticing your emotional reactions as part of your limiting life pattern cycle.

Emotional reactions are natural ways of responding to life's ups and downs, and they're especially pronounced when people don't do what you expect them to do or when situations don't go the way you want them to go. When you live in survival mode, you chase happiness outside of yourself and rely on others for your happiness. You wish and hope that one day, a person will show up, or people will change, or something will happen to finally make you happy. And every time you expect that moment to occur, with so much anticipation and hope, you give your power away to other people or other circumstances. You become vulnerable to whatever may or may not happen and keep adding more to your sandbags.

When you're blind to those sandbags and what they represent, you keep hovering at the lower levels of consciousness. Moreover, until you begin to learn about and reveal the vulnerable side of your psyche, your sandbags remain hidden. You know you're exposed to others' behaviors and attitudes and your emotional and mental balance heavily depend on outside circumstances. Even though they may not be favorable for you, you keep these people around or stay in situations longer than you should.

At lower consciousness levels you rely on your survival mechanisms, contracting your comfort zone even tighter to hide your vulnerability by having certain relationships, acquiring certain assets, pursuing certain careers, or hanging out with certain friends. Even so, you live in fear that your secrets will be discovered by them. In that powerless "victim" state, you keep engaging in limiting life patterns in which people or situations provoke your vulnerability even more by taking your power and happiness away.

As discussed earlier, you can't unconsciously and defensively run away from these patterns. Decoding your subconscious internal programming and discovering and releasing your sandbags, one by one, is the only way to bring the change within you that makes you feel lighter and more powerful. This process eventually brings the change you desire in people as they respond differently to the shift in your consciousness, which eventually changes your circumstances as well. That's how you find your true romance, your fulfilling career, your close friends, your community, and your purpose in life.

**Law of Life #2:
Life is not meant to be heavy or
confusing. Sandbags make it so.**

Going back to our hot air balloon analogy, imagine those rides as gentle, joyful, unforgettable adventures that allow you to see the world from a new perspective. When you sign up to go on one, you don't expect the ride to be bumpy or so laden with sandbags that you sail low to the ground, risking entanglement with power lines and treetops—in other words, be subject to highly intense and frequent limiting life patterns. On other occasions, weather patterns beyond your control might interfere with your ability to soar—or even force you to postpone your flight, as you may depend too much on outer circumstance based on the limitations your subconscious internal programming imposes. But your innate calling is to soar toward your highest potential. Life wants you to break free from the lower consciousness and experience Ultimate Happiness. That's exactly why you want to focus on decoding your subconscious internal programming. Expect to soar when you identify and separate yourself from your limiting life patterns. You will feel a sense of loftiness and freedom, along with the ability to shift direction when necessary, just as the balloon pilot responds to changing wind currents.

The first step to decoding your subconscious internal programming is to notice your emotional reactions.

CHAPTER TWO

PAUSING TO NOTICE YOUR EMOTIONS

Looking back, I realize now how many sandbags used to weigh me down without my conscious awareness. I constantly had intense emotional reactions in my life. In traffic, I would erupt in rage when a slow driver would hold up traffic in the fast lane. I used sarcastic, demeaning tones out of frustration when my partner disagreed with me on how to do things around the house. I was angry and condescending whenever my boss asked me when my presentation would be ready or demanded that I work another weekend. I froze out of anxiety and nervousness when I dined out at fine restaurants and didn't know how to act or what to order. I felt shame and wanted to run away when colleagues challenged my work and questioned my opinions in front of my boss. I curled up, hunched over, and felt a sense of self-pity and powerlessness when my mom extensively controlled my actions, disregarding my time and space, and when my dad dismissed me, unwilling to listen to what I had to say.

I don't know how many times I lost myself in these, and countless other, limiting life patterns, but I do know that, in each and every case, I reacted to people and situations without any control over my actions. They just happened as if someone or something else was in charge of me.

IDENTIFYING YOUR SANDBAGS

We all have sandbags, and they often show up in our day-to-day lives, manifesting in our emotional reactions to limiting life patterns. Identifying them is fundamental to decoding our subconscious selves, and the following practice will help you figure out where the sandbags in your life might be.

Life Skills Assignment #1:
Evaluate your life.

Pause for a minute from your busy life and take a look at this list. How satisfied or fulfilled do you feel in the following areas of your life?

Life Evaluation Form

A score of 1 means you're completely unhappy, dissatisfied, and unfulfilled; a score of 10 represents your complete happiness, satisfaction, and fulfillment. Just write N/A if the category doesn't apply.

Areas of Life

Physical Health   _____
Significant Other/Romance   _____
Kids   _____
Parents (Dad)   _____
Parents (Mom)   _____
Siblings   _____
Friends   _____
Fun and Recreation   _____
Money   _____
Career   _____
Time in Nature   _____
Personal Growth   _____
Fulfillment   _____

How did you do? I find this practice to be a very powerful self-reflection tool; it provides an opportunity for introspection about where you are in your life today and sheds some light on where the majority of your sandbags may be hiding. The lower your score on the life evaluation form, the more sandbags you potentially have. Even if you are thrown off by your lower score, remember that it only means you have some sandbags you need to discover and address.

Your honesty in answering this form will pay huge dividends in the future. Notice any category where you rated 6 or lower; that score may indicate the existence of heavy sandbags in that area, part of your life where you may be experiencing intense and frequent limiting life patterns. However, it's important to note that you may fill this form out differently on different days, depending on your mood and what's happening in your life. Since you will be addressing your sandbags throughout the following pages, I highly encourage you to come back to this practice from time to time and evaluate your life again.

UNDERSTANDING THE LIMITING LIFE PATTERN CYCLE

As mentioned earlier, in order to identify your sandbags and decode your subconscious, you need to become aware of your emotional reactions during those limiting life patterns that run a regular, intelligible cycle. Through the study of this cycle, you will gain access to valuable information, self-knowledge that will help you decipher that internal programming.

What does a typical limiting life pattern look like?

Cycles often start with a trigger: something or someone pushing your buttons and provoking your emotional reactions. Even though the trigger is the initiator of a limiting life pattern cycle, you usually notice your emotional reactions first. These reactions are actually a result of your perception, or how you saw and interpreted the trigger, and this perception depends on your subconscious internal programming, which drives how you react and launch your defensive actions.

Basically, your fight-or-flight response system automatically fires up your defenses to protect you against the trigger, a perceived threat. Your subconscious knows where you're vulnerable—where your sandbags lay hidden—and it knows you need help. This help often shows up in the form of aggressive, passive-aggressive, or passive defensive actions. But these defensive actions or strategies usually end up draining, and maybe even depleting, your energy reserves. That's when you feel exhausted, whether for a short moment or for months on end. You might fall into a state of conflict or confusion, and you start to question the partner you're with, the relationship you're in, the job you have, or even your overall career path or family umbrella. You might find yourself asking the question, *Shall I stay or shall I go?* The confusion lingers for a while, until things cool down a little bit. You forget some of the argument or the reason why you were triggered in the first place. You settle back into your familiar way of life. Time passes and everything somehow goes back to normal, as if nothing happened. Until the next trigger arises and kicks off the limiting life pattern cycle again.

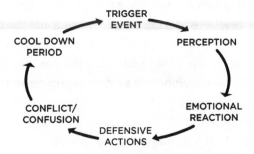

Where are the sandbags in this cycle?

I remember one time my boss had been very critical of my work, and, for a short period of time, I was under his close scrutiny. The night before a board meeting, I emailed him the slides I was going to present the following day. He texted me back in fifteen minutes.

"We need to talk asap!" There was my trigger.

I felt a cold chill run down my body, and my heart started to beat faster and louder. I was having an anxiety attack—this was my emotional reaction.

I was worried about what his message meant. He was probably going to tell me I had failed to include this or that in the presentation. It was 10:30 at night; what did he expect me to do? Should I call him to ask what he meant? But I was exhausted after putting that presentation together, and I didn't have the energy to take his criticism or have an unpleasant conversation with him.

At least this was my perception of what that conversation would have looked like. It was this perception, and the sandbag behind the perception, that weighed me down and led to this unhealthy state of anxiety.

So I went to bed, and that was my defensive action. It was my usual passive defensive action: avoidance and withdrawal. But it certainly didn't solve the problem, as defensive actions never do. Of course, I woke up in the middle of the night, again perspiring and short of breath, imagining how he would criticize my work, as usual, and how I would tell him that I was resigning before he could fire me. As I ruminated about these possibilities, I realized I couldn't possibly stay in that hostile work environment any longer. This was another defensive action, a passive-aggressive one: pushing away people by judging them and putting them down. I fell back to sleep again, now exhausted by all these thoughts.

When I hesitantly and reluctantly called him around 7:30 the next morning, on my way to work, I was not prepared for his reaction. To my shock, he started talking about my presentation favorably. He thanked me for the hard work I had put into it and told me what a great job I'd done in preparing the slides for the board meeting. You'd think I'd have run off the road with elation and relief. And his text the night before? Well, he had wanted to inquire about a minor detail missing in the presentation, one that he figured out later by himself. When I hung up, I noticed how tightly clenched my jaw was, along with my hands on the steering wheel. By the time I finally got to the office, my body had relaxed slightly, and I'd nearly forgotten all about it. I was ready to present at the meeting.

My limiting life pattern had become so habitual by this time in my life that I often cycled through it quickly—reacting, hurting, and recovering—as if it were an automatic cycle in a washing machine. The next step in the cycle was the cool down period that I enjoyed for a while, until my boss made another controversial comment, causing me another anxiety attack.

The key to decoding the subconscious and learning to rise above it is being able to recognize our perceptions, because that's where the sandbags lie hidden. Whether or not my boss had intended to appear threatening, or thought of my work poorly, it was my *perception*, based on other recent experiences with him, that he was angry and critical and I was in trouble. This is how my internal subconscious programming colored the situation and influenced how I reacted to his text, in terms of both emotional reactions and defensive actions.

DISCOVERING YOUR PERCEPTIONS

You take triggers personally because your perceptions tell you to do so. Behind every perception lies a thought pattern, a belief system, and a personal value set. Your subconscious internal programming consists of these thoughts, beliefs, and values, which constantly feed your perceptions, in the same way that coded instructions feed your computer's operating system. Your perceptions then dictate exactly how to interpret a certain situation, just as your operating system calls up a particular application depending on the instructions and the input. And finally, you derive meaning, whether true or false, from your life experiences based on your perceptions just as you derive capacity, productivity, or output from the application your computer's operating system presented to you.

You don't typically change your perceptions throughout your life, unless you proactively, consciously choose to work on them. For example, you may have felt abandoned when you were four years old and had to spend a month in the hospital alone, too young to understand why your mom couldn't stay with you. Then, later on, when you were in elementary school, you may have felt the same abandonment when your mom was half an hour late to pick you up, and you were the only kid waiting in the school yard. And more life experiences that provoked the same feeling of abandonment followed—when your boyfriend broke up with you in high school, when another boyfriend at college cheated on you, and when your first husband left you after many years together. Throughout these experiences, going through these limiting life patterns over and over again, your perceptions that you'll eventually be abandoned and that you can't trust people have been reinforced.

Even though your perceptions are subjective, they're based on your life experiences and are, therefore, very personal and unique to you. They are the lenses through which you look at life. You hide your vulnerability behind these perceptions, keeping your sandbags buried. Like in our example above, if you have a feeling that you'll be abandoned and can't trust people, you'd be very cautious in meeting people. But as far as the System of Life goes, you can't keep your sandbags buried forever. You'll meet people, and even though they may look trustworthy in the beginning, sooner or later, they will abandon you, and once again Life will invite you to look inward to explore your perceptions. When you don't question or challenge or consciously look at your thought patterns, belief systems, and value sets, you keep responding to situations and people the same way, using the same lens that your perceptions have been providing you for your entire life.

So does that mean you should change your perceptions?

Perhaps counterintuitively, the answer is no. Decoding subconscious internal programming requires that you keep your perceptions intact so you can discover them first, and then understand them thoroughly. If you change them to something more positive or more acceptable, you will end up reprogramming your subconscious, creating yourself another tight comfort zone for safety and protection.

On the contrary, decoding the subconscious and discovering your perceptions are about deeply understanding them, not about changing them. If you attempt to force a change in perception, or your underlying thoughts, beliefs, and values, for that matter, you will lose the connection to your sandbags and will not understand why they were there in the first place. In a sense, you can view this process as a decode, instead of a recode, and you will reach a point where your true essence naturally emerges in the process. You can then consciously gain the power back from your perceptions and create space for your authenticity, your Real Self, to show up—not as a recoded identity or persona that you created, but as a naturally true expression of your Self.

Let's explore this concept further using the computer-programming analogy we used earlier. Imagine you're a software engineer. You wrote some code. You turn the computer on, and your program starts to run, but what you see on the screen is gibberish, some unintelligible content. There are bugs in your code. What should you do when you don't like what you see on the screen? Would you cover the screen with a piece of paper? Would you paint the screen with a different, maybe brighter color? Would you disconnect the computer so that you didn't need to see that screen ever again?

What would you do?

If you attempt to alter the display, you may not be able to access the bugs in the code. Just as a computer screen reflects the software program running in the background, your defensive actions and emotional reactions are the result of thought patterns, belief systems, and value sets that lie beneath your perceptions. Instead of replacing these with new ones, the long-term solution for rising above your limiting patterns begins with decoding your internal source code. In other words, you start by trying to understand *why* you think and behave the way you do. In a way, decoding your subconscious internal programming is a reverse-engineering process in which you use the information you see on the computer screen—in this case, your emotional reactions and defensive actions—to decode your source code—all those thoughts, beliefs, and values stored in your subconscious. You're not trying to reprogram, but rather to understand.

In other words, you can't expect to extricate yourself from the limiting life pattern cycle by changing your thought patterns, belief systems, or value sets without deeper insight as to how they manifest in your limiting life patterns. Otherwise you might wind up with a program still full of bugs. But by reverse engineering your complex internal system, you will discover your basic survival system, with its fight-or-flight response, and you'll see how it suppresses another intrinsic system—the innate intellectual part of you that naturally strives for higher consciousness. You will see the ins and outs of your internal programming. You will come to know why you've formed your thought patterns, belief systems, and value sets the way you have. And you will then be able to slowly eliminate your dependence on the subconscious survival system and naturally begin to access the innate intelligence of higher consciousness.

In the lower levels of consciousness—the lower altitudes for a balloon laden with heavy sandbags—there are more bugs in your code, which means your subconscious internal programming is more sensitive to external threats. When operating at that level, you're more likely to take things personally and fire up your defensive actions quickly. Your limiting life patterns are often intense and frequent at this level. But as you work to understand, or decode, your subconscious programming, you will find your sandbags slowly releasing, and you'll sense a natural rise toward higher levels of consciousness and smoother sailing.

Linda and Chris haven't had a dinner date since they had their first baby eleven months ago, and now they've decided

the time has come. Both are very excited and have been looking forward to this night for weeks. Linda dresses up, and
they make their way to the restaurant. They review the menu
together like a romantic, newly dating couple, and after they
choose their favorite dish, they start catching up with each
other—something they haven't had a chance to do in a long
time.

While they are chitchatting, Chris's phone buzzes. He
immediately gets distracted. He keeps looking at his phone
while Linda is still talking to him. Linda notices his distraction and gets upset, having told him so many times before how
much it annoys her that he doesn't pay attention to her when
she's talking. She thinks Chris doesn't care about her and is
not willing to change his behavior to accommodate her needs.
Over and over again, they end up in this same situation, and
now on this romantic, once-in-a-long-while dinner date, there
he is checking his phone again.

Linda's blood starts to boil. She can't believe he would do
that on a night like this. "Can you put your phone down?"

"I'm just checking a message from a friend. Stop controlling
me. Enough already."

Although Linda is about to lose it, she manages to collect
herself. "How many times do I need to tell you, Chris? You
don't pay enough attention to me. I'm sick and tired of your
inconsiderate behavior."

Chris lifts his face from his phone. "That's not true. How
about the other day, when you were telling me about your
friends at work? I was giving you all the attention you needed.
You never appreciate *me* for the things I do. You always find
fault in me."

This back-and-forth argument goes on for nearly a half
hour, until their meal arrives. With no possible resolution in
sight, they eat their dinner silently, and they head home earlier
than they'd anticipated at the beginning of the night. When

they get there, Linda is frustrated and exhausted. They both give each other the silent treatment as they fall into bed. The conflict between them is so intense, so palpable, that Linda starts to think about whether this relationship can last, or even whether she made the right choice in the first place. The next morning, no one addresses what happened the night before, but things seem to have cooled down, and somehow their interactions normalize again as the day progresses. Until the next time, when Chris gets distracted by his phone again.

You just witnessed a typical limiting life pattern cycle. Did you notice each component of the pattern on full display? Let's investigate the situation scene-by-scene.

First, the trigger: Linda notices Chris checking his cell phone. That information is sent to her subconscious to evaluate and interpret according to her internal programming—her thought patterns, belief systems, and value sets. Milliseconds later, her subconscious whispers into her mind. *Chris is not interested in what you have to say.*

Second component, the perception: Linda believes Chris is losing interest in her. *He may even be interested in somebody else! Maybe I'm too boring. Whatever the case, he doesn't seem to value me as much, especially now that I spend so much time with our baby.*

Third phase, the emotional reaction: Heat runs through her veins as she gets angry.

Next, the defensive actions: Initially, she's aggressive, asking him to put his phone down with a sharp-edged tone. Then she becomes passive-aggressive, sarcastically asking how many times she has to tell him to pay attention to her.

Their brief back-and-forth clash, along with the subsequent restless night of ruminations about whether Chris is the right partner for her, illustrates the conflict/confusion stage of Linda's limiting life pattern cycle. And then, when she and

Chris settle into their normal lives and daily tasks the following morning, her cool down period begins.

Let's pause here.

Law of Life #3:
Only those who have sandbags react emotionally.

LEARNING TO PAUSE

How do you unpack all of this? How can you break free from this vicious cycle of a limiting life pattern?

By noticing your emotional reactions. As we've discussed, decoding your internal programming starts with identifying these reactions because they are the tip of an iceberg, the visible part of your subconscious internal programming. Noticing them allows you to use them as a reference point from which you can navigate a deeper journey of reverse engineering.

Granted, becoming aware of them can be difficult because your emotional reactions are often mind-blowingly fast. Sometimes it's a matter of only milliseconds. But when you learn to PAUSE, you find it easier to see your emotional reactions. You start to become more aware of when you're caught up in a limiting life pattern cycle. Through this awareness, you can slow down your thoughts and your actions, which eventually creates enough subtle space between you, what's going on in your head, and what's happening around you that you can view your subconscious internal programming right in front of you as if on a computer screen, ready to be decoded.

Life Skills Assignment #2:
Notice your emotional reactions.

Start a review practice at the end of each day, spending just five to ten minutes writing down one of your emotional reactions from that day. For the first few days, you may notice that your emotional reactions are all over the place. Or you may find that your days fly by, and you don't remember how you reacted to your triggers. And that's OK! This state is a testament to how we all have so many triggers each day and live under the reign of our subconscious internal programming, which, by design, has to invoke the fight-or-flight response quickly. It's natural that you don't always have time to become aware of what's going on around you, what you are saying, how you are acting, and what your emotions are. Or that you even feel out of control.

But now, beginning with learning to PAUSE, you're taking control back. You're shifting the decision-making process from the reactive, reptilian brain to the neocortex, where we are more aware of our actions and their consequences, and we understand why we do the things we do. With practice, you will begin to notice whenever you have an emotional reaction during the day. When this happens, slow down and bring your emotional reaction into your awareness by using the phrase *I am ____ now*. You can fill in the blank with any emotion arising as a result of a trigger. The more you become aware of your emotional reactions during the day, the better you will remember them for your daily review at night.

SLOWING THINGS DOWN

How do you slow down so that you can be more aware of your emotional reactions?

Through *self-observation meditation*. The purpose of this type of meditation is to sharpen your ability to concentrate and hold your focus for longer times so that you can observe the busyness of your mind. It's different from other meditation techniques, where the goal may be to get rid of negative, intruding, or cluttering thoughts and relax. In this meditation, you practice observing when you're under the control of your subconscious and creating a new presence, rather than trying to change how your subconscious operates.

Self-observation meditation, in other words, is a mental practice that improves your ability to step back from a situation and witness it from a distance with detachment and indifference. It allows you to slow your thoughts down and create an expanded awareness. You use this tool to generate a space between you and your mind, helping you consciously see and understand your own thoughts and behaviors.

A cloud metaphor can help explain self-observation meditation. Imagine you're on a green, grassy hill having a picnic on a beautiful spring day. Above you, clouds slowly and gently float against blue skies. Sometimes, you see a shape form in the clouds. A dolphin, a rabbit, a lion. How do you tend to observe them? Are you indifferent, or do you tend to get sucked into stories about these shapes?

Self-observation meditation is similar. Imagine your thoughts, feelings, or physical sensations as if they were clouds floating through the sky. Sometimes they're dark, heavy, and angry. Sometimes they're light, cheerful, and calm. But whichever type of clouds they might be, they are separate from you, the individual simply observing them. In this type of meditation practice, you are an impartial, detached, objective observer who acknowledges thoughts, feelings, and physical sensations without engaging in them. You may occasionally get lost in your thoughts and emotions and physical pain; this is normal, but when this happens, it means your subconscious is trying to take back control. What should you do when that happens? Simply acknowledge that you are lost! Then slowly bring your attention back to yourself—back to the picnic on a grassy hill—and start observing as a third-party witness again.

Life Skills Assignment #3:
Practice self-observation meditation.

It's time to practice. Start by choosing a location where you won't be interrupted while you practice, and then set a timer. If you're new to these types of practices, you might want to start with just three minutes. Yes, just three minutes a day will be enough to train yourself to take over your attention and focus. Of course, you can add more time later, when you feel more comfortable with the process.

Sit on a comfortable chair with your knees at a ninety-degree angle and your feet flat on the floor. Your back, neck, and head should be aligned. If the chair has a back, move forward toward the center of the chair so that your back doesn't rest on it; otherwise, you may get too comfortable and slouch or even fall asleep. If you have to lean your back on the chair, that's OK too, but in that case, keep your back straight to help create a sense of presence. Your goal should be to relax your body as much as you can while maintaining a posture that's erect without being rigid or strained.

Place your hands on your lap, one on top of the other, palms up, fingers pointing in opposite directions, one resting on the other, without interlocking. Next, bring your thumbs together, creating a circle, and let them softly touch each other on their meaty tips, while being careful not to press too hard. In this pose, you are creating a basket where your palms represent the container and your thumbs the handle. Let your arms relax.

Now take a deep breath in, and as you exhale, close your eyes. Keep your mouth closed and breathe naturally. Bring your focus to the light touch of your thumbs, noticing the tangible, physical sensation that your thumbs create. Hold your attention there as long as you can. Only a few seconds after you place your focus on your thumbs, your thoughts will try to steal your attention away from them. Initially you won't even notice when this happens. You will softly drift into daydreaming. Soon you'll find yourself swimming in mind chatter: your thoughts, stories, interpretations of what happened today, plans for the evening, worries, and emotional reactions to this person or that situation will all show up. The physical sensation of your thumbs, along with your attention on the sensation and your commitment to stay focused, will be long gone.

Well, no worries. Your practice actually begins right there. It's OK if you're feeling frustrated or your body starts to itch. It's OK if you can't even sit still for thirty seconds. When this happens, just try to observe what you're thinking and feeling at that moment, paying attention to the images in your mind. And if even that feels like an elusive task, that's OK too. That's what self-observation meditation is all about: learning to catch yourself lost in thought, noticing the busyness of your mind and whatever you're feeling in head, heart, and body, and ultimately developing the ability to regain control. Be patient and gentle with yourself. It *will* happen.

When your time has ended, finish your practice by taking another deep breath and exhaling slowly. Then open your eyes, release your hands and thumbs, and notice how you feel.

How often should you practice self-observation meditation? I recommend at least once a day. For me, the best time is right after I wake up—before diving into the busyness of my day. Feel free to experiment with different times throughout the day to find what works best for you. You may also want to try practicing twice a day—once in the morning and once before you go to bed at night—or slipping in a one-minute practice here and there throughout the day—between meetings, errands, or meals—or even when you're waiting for the red light to turn green.

REASONS BEHIND YOUR EMOTIONS

We've been talking about how to identify and observe our emotions, but let's take a step back and dig into why we have emotions. According to Lisa Feldman Barrett, the author of *How Emotions Are Made: The Secret Life of the Brain* and a neuroscientist who has researched emotions for the last twenty-five years, emotions are predictions. They're constructed by the brain and based on your past experiences in order to make sense of everything that is currently happening around you.

Your emotions are always provoked by a stimulus. The moment your brain senses a potential threat, which I call a trigger because it kicks off the limiting life pattern cycle, your attention is directed outward to assess the situation and ward off a possible threat to your safety. For these purposes, safety can involve your physical well-being in addition to your emotional, mental, or spiritual state. In the blink of an eye, you lose conscious control and your subconscious takes over, hooking you back into the cycle to defend against the perceived threat.

But now that you've been practicing self-observation meditation, you're ready to take the next step and PAUSE when triggers come along and provoke your emotions. As with the meditation practice, you get hold of your attention and turn it inward. By doing so, you can begin to notice more specific details about your triggers, as well as their ripple effects in your head and in your body.

**Life Skills Assignment #4:
Notice the triggers that provoke
emotional reactions.**

Whenever you pause to notice your emotions, can you also discern why you feel that emotion? For example, you notice you're feeling upset. You PAUSE. Now ask yourself, *What made me feel upset?* Learning more about your triggers is fundamental to becoming unstuck and moving forward on your journey to Ultimate Happiness. I recommend incorporating a trigger assignment into your daily review. Here's an example of what it might look like.

> Today's Date: July 24, 2020
> 1. Emotion: Upset.
> 2. Trigger: My friend invited my best friend
>   for a drink, but not me.

Repeat this assignment for a week or so and then review what you've identified as triggers. If a particular trigger repeats regularly, ask yourself what might be underlying it, and notice how the limiting life pattern cycle plays out because of it. The list below summarizes some common triggers you may encounter in your life. You may notice that they occasionally contradict each other, either because they reflect different meanings for different people or because the triggers, in general, aren't always mutually exclusive and can overlap. If some of these examples look familiar to you, watch for them over the coming days and track them in your daily reviews.

People as Triggers
(underline the ones that are applicable to you)

My Partner

Puts down whatever I do, whatever I say. Blames me for everything. Interrupts me or talks over me all the time. Ignores my needs and feelings. Doesn't see me, hear me. Doesn't partake in any housework or childrearing. Eats, drinks, smokes too much. Doesn't appreciate what I do for them. Doesn't want to do the things I want to do. Watches TV all the time. Is not affectionate with me. Thinks I'm incapable of handling things. Flirts with others, disregarding my presence. Hangs out with their friends too much. I feel like I don't even have a partner. I don't have anyone to spend the weekends with.

My Child

Rejects, ignores, or negotiates when asked to do something. Doesn't get along with others. Doesn't appreciate what I do for them. Eats a lot—or doesn't eat enough. Doesn't learn as fast as other kids. Doesn't show much affection toward me or want to be close with me. Undermines my authority. Requires a lot of my personal time. Says hurtful things when angry at me. Acts out in front of others. Is overscheduled with school/sports activities. Nags me all the time to buy them toys, games, clothes. Has unhealthy habits.

My Boss

Doesn't appreciate my hard work. Never praises me or recognizes my contribution. Constantly dismisses or ignores my ideas and suggestions. Criticizes and sometimes mocks me in front of others. Takes credit for my work and ideas. Throws me under the bus. Doesn't invite me to important meetings. Micromanages me. Interrupts me in meetings. Is very hands-off, doesn't pay attention to details. Doesn't give much direction. Asks me to work more hours. Is very demanding, with no respect for my personal time.

My Colleague

Is neither collaborative nor cooperative. Takes credit for my work, my ideas. Never agrees with my suggestions. Always dumps their work on me. Just got promoted to a position I deserved. Doesn't include me in work meetings or social meetings. Gossips and constantly talks behind my back, badmouths me. Has a negative attitude toward me. Throws me under the bus whenever they get criticized. Constantly sucks up to management.

My Parents

Expect me to be perfect. Pressure me to do the things they want. Compare me to others. Don't pay much attention to me. Constantly criticize my actions and the way I think and live. Need my attention all the time. Are in my business, constantly giving me unsolicited advice. Have no expectations of me, completely ignore me. Never ask about my personal life. Think that I'm incapable of handling things. Criticize my significant other, friends. Verbally attack me. Are distant, not nurturing people. Never call me.

My Friend

Never asks how I'm doing. Doesn't appreciate what I do for them. Always asks for favors. Flirts with my significant other. Doesn't include me in their plans. Constantly criticizes my actions and my thoughts; tries to give me advice. Drains my energy. Is a very negative person. Doesn't call me back in time. Is flaky, can't trust them. Always talks about their drama, their issues. Gossips and talks behind my back. Is very selfish, needy, demanding. Is only engaged when they want something from me. I don't seem to connect with my friends. I don't have any friends. I still feel lonely when I'm around my friends.

Situations as Triggers
(underline the ones that are applicable to you)

News

The news is cluttered with so many horrible things happening in the world. I don't understand why politicians don't get along and collaborate for the collective benefit of people. Wherever I look, there is bad news. Everybody on TV seems to be shouting. Sensationalism makes me withdraw from life.

Social Media

I don't understand why everyone on social media needs to share how great their life is. Why do I need to know what someone ate for dinner? I can't stop scrolling down the feed, even though it feels empty. I stay up late being curious about how others are doing.

Dating

I don't think there is anybody out there for me as a romantic partner. I don't want to meet people at bars or clubs anymore. All the good ones are taken. I feel like a loser every time I go on a date and it turns out to not be the right person. Why do I keep attracting losers? I don't want to write my profile and brag about myself. I'm too private to date. I don't trust men. I don't trust women. I'm not sure if I'm in a committed dating situation here. I'm dating a couple of people, and I'm not sure which one(s) I should let go. Everyone is so superficial;

no one wants to get serious. I hate being ghosted. Everyone lies on their profile. Everyone is so rude and disrespectful.

Job Interview

I have no experience or qualifications to find a good job. I don't think I got the job I just interviewed for; they didn't seem to like my answers. I have no idea how to prepare for this upcoming interview. I was so nervous; I'm sure I bombed the interview. I don't like to promote myself or to talk about myself. I don't interview well. I hate interviews. I have no self-confidence. I don't present myself well. I don't think they liked me. I need to take more certification courses to feel qualified and be ready for my next job.

Too much to do

I can't say no to people, so I take on more and more. My job is too demanding. I do a lot of housework. I have too much to do and don't have enough time for myself. Everyone is relying on me. I don't know how to set healthy boundaries. I give too much and receive too little. Too many meetings. Nobody respects my time.

Traffic

Someone cut me off on the freeway, again! Reckless drivers are everywhere. Someone is always on the phone, texting, while driving. There are too many cars on the road. Nobody waits for three seconds at the stop sign. No parking spots are ever available. I always run into bad traffic. Slow drivers always find me, especially when I have to be somewhere in half an hour. Someone cursed at me and flipped *me* off. Someone is tailgating, driving too close to me. Someone honked at me because I was one second too slow when the light turned green. There is too much traffic!

Health

I don't pay attention to my health as much as I should. I don't keep my promises to eat healthy, exercise more, drink less, be active, or spend time in nature. I stay up so late that I don't get enough sleep. Why can't I go for a fifteen-minute walk between meetings at work? I'm so obsessed with my health that I get checkups too frequently. I run multiple marathons every year. I love the way I look. I hate the way I look. I like getting attention. I don't understand why some people are not health-conscious and don't take care of themselves.

Job/Career

I'm overwhelmed because I don't know what I want to do in my career. I can't focus on my job. I feel unmotivated, uninspired. No one seems to be doing their job properly. I've lost respect for my profession. I have trouble completing projects. I feel lost: shall I do what brings me financial stability or something that brings me joy?

Money

I never have enough money. When am I going to get promoted? I want to make more money. So many bills to pay. I don't have enough saved for the future. I spend too much whenever I go out. Everybody seems to be well-off except me. They don't pay me enough. Where is my abundance? I don't like my job but have to stay for the money. I don't seem to attract money—what's wrong with me? I can't manage my money well. I speculate in the financial markets a lot. I love gambling.

Public Speaking

I don't feel like an expert on the subject that I'm about to give a talk about. I don't like talking in front of people. I can't command the room. I don't get enough eye contact from people. I don't have anything interesting to say. People seem to be preoccupied when I'm talking. I am so nervous standing in front of people. I feel like all eyes are on me. I'm afraid I'll stop talking in the middle of my presentation and forget what I need to say. I look like an idiot on stage.

So many triggers in life! So many people, so many situations, so many inner dialogues that act like triggers. We can't run away from them. They're everywhere. And you may have certainly either experienced some of these or know someone who has. After all, no one is exempt from triggers. Now that you've been introduced to, or reminded about, some potential triggers, keep an eye out for these as you work on your daily reviews in the coming weeks.

TRIGGERS AS MESSENGERS

Triggers are the people or situations that aggravate your Achilles' heel, poke at your vulnerability, and activate those sandbags that weigh you down to lower altitudes, no matter how happy you are or how high you've been flying. They deplete your energy. They exhaust your tank. They send you back into reacting emotionally, deploying defensive actions, and facing conflict and confusion. That's why you need to learn to PAUSE in the presence of these triggers, so you can understand them and develop a resilience against them.

And as irritating as they can be, triggers are actually here for a reason. They serve as an invitation to understand the root cause of your conflicts in life, be it at home, at work, in your relationships, in your career, or with your friends. But I certainly didn't know that for a long time—not as a teenager when my parents controlled and disciplined me, or as a young adult when my ex-wife criticized me, or even later on, when my boss failed to appreciate my work or when my friends ignored my career shift and never asked about my transformation. It wasn't until much farther into my journey that I was able to discern the true meaning of my life and what my triggers had been trying to reveal to me, layer by layer. And you'll discover this, too, as you walk along the same steps of the same journey of self-discovery.

Law of Life #4:
Triggers are the messengers of sandbags.

The message that each trigger delivers is a substantial one because every time you're triggered, you have a chance to learn about your Self. Armed with that new insight and awareness, you can decode even more of your subconscious internal programming and slowly release the sandbags—the vulnerabilities—that are holding you back.

CHAPTER THREE

OBSERVING YOUR THOUGHTS TO DECODE YOUR SUBCONSCIOUS

Have you noticed that you react to some triggers and not to others? Or that people react to circumstances differently? Why is that?

Let's say you meet your friend for coffee. She spends your entire time together complaining about her overly attentive boyfriend. You listen to her, but it doesn't make sense to you why it's such a big deal. You don't see a problem and try to counsel her.

"Don't worry about it; at least he pays attention to you. Look at my boyfriend. He doesn't care what I do. He doesn't ask where I've been. He completely dismisses me. You should let it go. Enjoy his attention. It's not a big deal!"

Yet your friend keeps complaining about her boyfriend and is now angry with you, too, for not understanding her or for taking his side.

This phenomenon can also show up in arguments between couples. One accuses the other, for example, of not caring about a difficult situation a friend is dealing with. And maybe it's true; maybe they don't. But whatever the case may be, the pair definitely doesn't understand each other's point of view or why two people who love each other can't be on the same page. Why are they not as triggered as each other? Why are you and your friend triggered by different things? As we've already seen, our perceptions are based on individual thought patterns, belief systems, and value sets, which are in turn based on our own personal histories and experiences. Our triggers will be aligned only if we *share similar histories and experiences.*

This is what perception is all about. Everyone looks at life through perceptions that are unique and specific to them. Like colored glasses, our perceptions influence how we see and receive the outside world and its impact on us.

And what gives these glasses their color?

Sandbags.

As we discussed earlier, sandbags represent our vulnerability. They're hidden in our subconscious internal programming. They weigh us down. They keep us from being happier. Because our vulnerability begins to form early in life, we each grow up seeing the world differently.

For example, I remember being scolded by my dad at a dinner at my Auntie's on a Sunday evening because I didn't know how to use their new state-of-the-art pepper mill. I felt so inadequate because of his admonishment that I was afraid to try new things for a long time afterward. Instead, I clung to my old, reliable comfort zone, where everyone and everything was familiar, and my vulnerability was protected. Even after growing up, I tended to shy away from new projects for fear I might receive a similar reaction from someone else. Eventually I grew so dependent on my comfort zone that I became trapped inside it.

Mark had a similar experience. He was scolded for wearing casual blue jeans and a flannel shirt to a formal family gathering when he was a teenager, and later he found himself triggered when his wife commented on how he was dressed for work.

"Are you going to wear *that* shirt to work today?" she asked.

Even though it was a simple question without any ulterior motive, he had learned from his childhood experience that he was bound by others' judgment on what was right or wrong, and he didn't even feel free to choose what to wear.

When Susie was a child, she was criticized by her parents for speaking up at the dinner table. Years later, she got triggered when she and her husband discussed school options for their children, and he didn't listen to her. She had learned from her childhood experience that she didn't have a voice and that her thoughts or opinions weren't important.

Yes, we all take trigger events personally because of our unique perceptions, influenced by years of thought patterns, belief systems, and value sets that came from our experiences and that became integral parts of the subconscious internal programming designed to protect us against possible outside threats. But just as our triggers reveal our vulnerability, our perceptions also hold the key to unlock the mysteries of our subconscious.

Law of Life #5:
Perceptions give meaning to your life experiences.

How do you discover your perceptions? By observing your thoughts when you're triggered in the same way you've learned to observe your emotional reactions. In a sense, your thoughts are the reflection of your perceptions. You can use both terms interchangeably.

For example, you may get annoyed when someone doesn't respond to your text message quickly enough. What is your thought then? You may *think* that your friend doesn't like you. How does that thought come to your mind? It appears courtesy of your subconscious internal programming: *When a friend doesn't text me for a day after I text them, that means they don't like me.* It's irrelevant whether this particular friend likes you; the conclusion drawn by your internal programming is based on past experience and becomes your perception. Like a computer, the subconscious works exactly like a logical algorithm: If X happens, then that means Y based on the past experience Z.

You see, the whole journey of self-discovery is nothing but a reverse-engineering process from the emotions to the thoughts, and from the thoughts to the perceptions, and from the perceptions to the thought patterns, belief systems, and value sets that served as the foundation for those perceptions. Once you start to pull the thread and reverse engineer the inner workings of your whole system, you will understand where your thought patterns, belief systems, and value sets—and the resultant perceptions—come from.

First you started noticing your emotions, then you became aware of your triggers, and now you are about to observe the thoughts that are in your head.

Life Skills Assignment #5:
Observe your thoughts.

Let's put all of this into practice. Whenever you have an emotional reaction, can you PAUSE to notice your emotions, become aware of what triggered you, and then immediately OBSERVE the thoughts going through your head?

There's a lot to accomplish in this practice. In the beginning, it can be difficult to stop in the middle of a heated exchange and immediately notice your emotions, the triggers, and your thoughts, all while trying to respond to the situation. Be patient. You will build your foundation for the POWER Method step-by-step over time, and one day you'll notice a positive shift or a sense of expanded space in the middle of an argument. For now, just keep trying to PAUSE and OBSERVE when you're triggered.

As part of this practice, use your daily review journal to record your thoughts about one of your trigger events each day in addition to naming your emotion and the trigger.

> Today's Date: March 12, 2020
> 1. Emotions: Anger. Impatience.
> 2. Trigger: It's morning. We're late to school. Kids are dragging their feet to get ready. One of them couldn't find one of their shoes.
> 3. Thought: This is too much work. They are going to be late. I'll be embarrassed.

One difficulty in this assignment might be turning your attention inward, toward your thoughts. Typically, when you're triggered, your attention turns outward toward the trigger. Of course, this defensive move is part of your survival mechanisms—you're looking outward to see if there's a threat. But when your attention pivots to the external, you become blind to your perceptions and inner thoughts. As a result, you miss critical information about how you perceive the situation and why it's a trigger for you. Without that knowledge, you take the situation personally and react emotionally.

Your thoughts reflect your vulnerability, and as we move forward you'll learn how to use those thoughts, the way a detective uses clues, to decode your subconscious internal programming. As you do, you'll look deeper into your survival mechanisms and pinpoint the instructions your mind receives from your subconscious. And you will discover the amazing root-cause-effect relationship that exists everywhere in life, including inside your own mind.

Law of Life #6:
A root-cause-effect relationship exists in all situations in life.

By design, the System of Life, the fabric of the matrix you live in, creates these relationships for you so you can navigate through the journey of self-discovery to go deeper within your subconscious internal programming and get to know your Self intimately. Only then can you consciously drop off the sand-bags that hold you down.

FINDING THE ROOT-CAUSE-EFFECT

I used to get anxious every time I went to dinner at a fine restaurant in downtown San Francisco. I would worry about whether I'd find a free parking spot on the street so I could avoid having to pay the twenty-dollar flat overnight rate at a parking garage. I thought it was a waste of money. Then I'd sit down for dinner, and as soon as my eyes landed on the menu's prices, I'd realize I would have to order pasta instead of delicious steak or fish because I thought that was all I could afford. Other times, I'd get overly excited whenever I received the tenth stamp on my local deli card and earned a free sandwich.

Opportunities to save money and be frugal always seemed important to me. What was this all about? I had a decent salary as a corporate controller at a high-tech company in Silicon Valley, but even so I suffered from this worry, this nervousness and apprehension around finances. Let's use our reverse-engineering process to understand how the root-cause-effect relationship showed up in my life. We'll start with the effect first, just to see how the relationship manifests. Then we'll dive deep into the cause and, finally, review the root of what's really happening underneath in my subconscious internal programming.

What was the effect? My emotional reactions and defensive actions were the effect from insisting on saving money at the expense of enjoying life. I was anxious. I was nervous. I felt inadequate, and all these emotional reactions depleted my energy. My defensive actions, which included extensive driving around while looking for free parking and depriving myself of the food I really craved, were passive-aggressive because I was actively avoiding having to face the situation directly. One day I became very angry at myself because I had parked on the street instead of a garage—to save twenty dollars—but then got a parking ticket because the parking was free after 6:00 p.m., not 5:00 p.m. I was so mad at myself that, even the following day, I walked around long-faced and grumpy, refusing to talk to anybody except one of my colleagues, whom I yelled at for almost no reason. I ate a bunch of cookies in the office, and then I was mildly depressed for the next few days, all because I had to pay seventy dollars for a parking violation.

What was the cause? My emotional reactions and defensive actions were caused by thought patterns that I had to save every penny, by a belief system that said life was very unpredictable and anything could happen any time, and by a value set that called for a financially secure future. Throughout my life, until I was able to release the sandbags related to this *cause*, I constantly thought about how much something cost and whether it was worth spending that much money, whether it was a $5 or $500 purchase.

What was the root? Right before I went to college, my dad left his lucrative manager position at a Turkish company to venture off on his own. A few years later, he declared bankruptcy when he didn't find it in himself to continue the rat race. At the time, we were living in Feneryolu, on the Asian side of Istanbul, and I was commuting to my school, Boğaziçi University, on the European side. It took me one and a half hours each way, and I had to choose between two different routes. Almost every day, trying to decide which way to go gave me headaches. One option was to use the bus-only route, which meant changing buses twice along the way and standing up for the entire time, packed in with other commuters like sardines. The other option was bus, ferry, and bus again. The ferry ride was leisurely, and it gave me the opportunity to sit down and enjoy the beautiful views of Istanbul. But it cost one and a quarter Turkish Lira more each way, which is about five US dollars in today's terms. And that was a big deal for me, as my family was financially struggling, which turned out to be the *root* of my behavior and challenges in life regarding my relationship with money. Even though I had well-paying corporate jobs later in life, this financial anxiety and worry about future financial instability stuck with me. It created my limiting life pattern of making daily decisions between saving or splurging, either making smart and frugal decisions about money or agonizing about those choices I made that were more extravagant.

My dad's sudden bankruptcy, and the change in our standard of living, added to my anxieties about life. We no longer ate out at restaurants. I was no longer able to attend tennis lessons at the local club, and my mom asked me to delay learning French at the Alliance Française d'Istanbul during the summers. We tried to be frugal when buying groceries. My parents started using coupons clipped out of the newspaper every Sunday to get kitchen appliances or cleaning supplies. To help my family, I started working the midnight shift at a credit card company, answering calls to give authorization numbers to vendors. For the first time in my life, I felt financial pressure and related anxiety, which became the root of all my thought patterns, belief systems, and value sets concerning money. They, in turn, caused my financial worries and led to corresponding limiting life patterns.

Because of these life experiences and the specific root-cause-effect relationship they created, I thought that nothing was certain and secure in life. I believed that anything could happen at any time and take away resources and bring hardship and difficulty into my life. As a result, I grew to value financial security above everything, which is probably the reason I chose a secure and predictable finance and accounting career after I graduated from college.

Let's explore these concepts further, checking in with Linda and Chris again. I think they're about to get into another argument.

You may recall that they'd had a fight about Chris checking his cell phone while Linda was trying to have a conversation with him. They'd gone to bed without making up, and the next morning brought a sense of being back to normal. But now it's the next evening, and Linda comes home from a stressful day at work. As usual, she grabs a glass of red wine and joins Chris in the kitchen to prepare dinner. While they're working on their respective tasks, Linda enthusiastically starts to tell Chris about the new hire on her team, and how happy she is with his performance so far. All of a sudden, Chris turns around.

"Why are you chopping the bell peppers like that?"

Linda abruptly stops her story, offended by Chris's interruption as well as his jab at how she's doing something she's done for years.

"Who gives you the right to criticize what *I* do in the kitchen, while you've been ignoring what I've told *you* so many times: not to put the wine glasses in the lower dishwasher tray? Remember the two broken wine glasses we've had in just the last couple of weeks?"

Let's pause here and use our reverse-engineering process again to get to the bottom of what's going on, first from Linda's perspective and then from Chris's.

What is the effect? One is Linda's emotional outburst about how Chris often interrupts her while talking, criticizes her, or makes snarky comments about something she does. The other effect is her defensive actions, her aggressive question that points out Chris's mistakes in the past, an effort to ward off the threat of being seen as not good enough, inadequate, and not valued.

What is the cause? The immediate cause of Linda's reaction was Chris's criticism of how she was chopping the bell peppers and her perception that, because she always excelled at everything she did, his criticism wasn't warranted. Linda thinks there's always a better way of doing things. She believes in hard and diligent work and in being perfect in what she does. Her top value is to strive for excellence in all areas of life. These thought patterns, belief systems, and values influencing her perceptions made her feel not good enough, inadequate, and not valued when she heard Chris criticize the way she chopped the bell peppers.

What is the root? Linda grew up as an only child in a scholarly home; both of her parents had PhDs. Her parents nitpicked any small mistakes she might make and, because they withheld praise from her, she worked hard to excel in everything she did, with the hope it would garner their praise and make them proud.

So the root of the problem from Linda's perspective was this: she had learned that excellence and being perfect in what you do is of paramount importance to being accepted, appreciated, and loved by others. By extension, criticism meant that she wasn't accepted, appreciated, or loved by Chris, or by her parents, who would question and criticize her for trivial things. As a result, every criticism, small or big, made her feel not good enough, inadequate, and not valued, causing her to emotionally react and aggressively defend her vulnerability.

Here's an interesting twist: Who do you think is triggered first? Chris or Linda? It's actually Chris. That's why Chris feels that he has to point out, passive-aggressively, how Linda is chopping the bell peppers. That's why he's using a sarcastic, judgmental question to put Linda down even though they are both having fun getting dinner ready.

His judgmental question—the passive-aggressive defensive action—is the *effect* you see in his behavior. He's emotionally reacting to Linda. He's frustrated with her and brings up a subjective point of view on a trivial matter to put Linda down.

Why does he do that? Why is he triggered? What is the *cause* of Chris's behavior?

Chris is triggered when Linda tells him about her day. Chris immediately feels not good enough, and less-than, even not worthy of Linda, when he listens to her go on and on about her new hire and how successful her team is. These feelings remind him of the old days, when all his parents talked about was how successful his older brother, Matt, was, and how much better Chris needed to be to catch up to his older brother.

When he's listening to Linda, his thought patterns of low self-worth and not being as good as she is are provoked. In addition, his belief system of being a loser no matter what, and never being able to find success in life, is confirmed. And the set of values of forming a warm, close, and intimate relationship is challenged by Linda's professional success because her job often takes her away from home and from him. Chris's perceptions make him feel like a loser, not good enough, abandoned, and worthless.

What is the *root* of these thought patterns, belief systems, and set of values?

Chris was the second child. Matt was three years older than he and accomplished everything before Chris. He was the quarterback on the high school football team and a very popular guy. He ran the fraternity house that everyone wanted to join. He also thrived academically, receiving respect and admiration from his teachers. In order to motivate Chris, his parents compared him to Matt, hoping that Chris could change his lifestyle and pull himself together, that he could find his place in the world. Chris thought he wasn't capable of doing anything, believed he wasn't good enough for anyone, and valued minding his own business and doing his own thing without trying to prove anything to his parents until he left town to study abroad, where he tried to find himself and his confidence.

DIVING DEEPER INTO THE ROOT

The emotional reactions and defensive actions are the *effects* of your perceptions. Conversely, the perceptions are the *cause*. They arise from your underlying thought patterns, belief systems, and value sets, which have evolved over time to protect your vulnerability and serve as your survival mechanisms. And the *root* is the vulnerability that stems from the initial life experiences that created certain emotional sensitivity in you. These elements of your subconscious internal programming aren't visible to you until you recognize the root-cause-effect relationship between each of them and how your emotional reactions and defensive actions come about.

Why would I drive around to avoid a twenty-dollar parking fee? Why would Chris feel less-than when listening to Linda's success? Why would Linda feel criticized when Chris asked a simple question? The answer is this: When we receive information that is, in essence, a repeat of our past experiences, our subconscious internal programming tells the mind to fire up our fight-or-flight response system, which then orders our emotions to activate and launch our defensive actions. It doesn't want us to have to live through the pain again—a pain that's been stored in our subconscious memories along with our vulnerability, as our sandbags.

The *root*, in other words, is the original feeling, the very first emotional hurt you experienced in the very first incident that provoked those emotional reactions and defensive actions, which have since repeated over and over as your limiting life patterns. The anxious worry I felt every morning when decid-ing which route I should take came from an original feeling. The unworthy feeling Linda experienced whenever her parents criticized her became the root of her emotional reactions. The feeling of less-than Chris dealt with in the shadow of his broth-er's accomplishments formed the root of why he felt threat-ened by Linda's success.

The root could be likened to a wound on your arm or even a papercut on your finger. The first time it happens, the pain is huge. The burning sensation is irritating. That's the first shock to your body. Then what happens? You put a Band-Aid on it. You cover it with your sweater. You try to be careful not to bump it anywhere and pull it back when someone gets close to it, fearing they will touch the wound and reignite the pain in your body. But, in reality, what happens? You keep bumping into the door, your car, your bed. You sometimes hit it yourself. You keep swearing as you wonder why this keeps happening, yet it does. Life is the same, whether it's physical or emotional or psychological pain. The first time you're triggered, you feel the pain of the new wound, and then limiting life patterns start to arise, and each additional time you face another trigger, you experience that accidental touch on your wound that hurts as much as the first time, because no matter what you do to cover it, it's still there.

LIFE'S UNEXPECTED PLANS

Well, what happens to those original feelings, the wounds? We often don't have the necessary tools to recognize and process those deep, hurtful feelings when the wound first occurs. Even as adults, we sometimes don't know how to address complex feelings or express what's happening internally. All we know is that we feel vulnerable, helpless, and powerless, and we don't like that feeling, so we run away from it, cover the wound, and avoid it at all costs. Yes, of course, being vulnerable is frightening, painful, and scary. So we block and suppress those wounds, those original feelings. We bury them in our subconscious, hoping to never see them again. And as they lay buried, they become *repressed fears*.

Maybe at one time you experienced original feelings of not being good enough, not being valued, and so on, so you've avoided people who tend to criticize, or who devalue your opinions, or who make you feel smaller. Maybe you still avoid people who dismiss your presence, don't hear what you're saying, ignore you, or put you down. Yet you still keep running into them. If this is the case, it might be that this is one of your limiting life patterns, and your triggers are the messengers for your sandbags, your vulnerability, your repressed fears. It might be that one of life's unexpected missions for *you* is to reveal your sandbags through your triggers so you can recognize and process your repressed fears. So you can break free from your vulnerability. So you can release your sandbags and rise above your pain and realize Ultimate Happiness.

Your repressed fears are the root of everything.

You can find your sandbags beneath every emotional reaction, and that's why you start the reverse-engineering process by noticing your emotions, at the tip of the iceberg. Then you become aware of those triggers that provoked your emotional reactions. After that, you slowly work your way into your inner programming and start observing your thoughts. Now you're ready to go even deeper into the root cause, into those repressed fears that influence your thoughts—and your entire life.

How do you identify your repressed fears?
Through an internal investigation. You are about to deepen your exploration of your survival mechanisms, and their complex structure, and in so doing find out what's going on behind

the scenes when you emotionally react to a trigger. Put your Sherlock Holmes hat on and join me on this exciting journey that takes us one step closer to Ultimate Happiness.

How do you conduct an internal investigation?

An effective tool in the reverse-engineering process, internal investigation challenges your thoughts through a series of questions that ask *"what if—so what."* Your goal is to dig deeper until you reach a worst-case scenario: the exact situation that your repressed fears want you to avoid. Right after that first incident, your repressed fears cautioned you: *Prevent all future situations that are potentially as painful as this one.* But what happens? You keep experiencing the triggers that remind you of that first incident, so that you go inward and find out about your repressed fears. That's why your limiting life patterns come into play. The moment a trigger provokes your emotional reactions, that's the perfect time to conduct your internal investigation.

I distinctly remember a specific limiting life pattern that happened frequently throughout my corporate career, and it always went something like this: I'm in a weekly meeting with five or six colleagues and my boss. A question arises about the expense-reporting process and how the managers approve the reports. I suggest an idea to streamline it. Neither my boss nor my colleagues seem to notice my suggestion. And then, when one of my colleagues proposes an idea that's almost exactly what I suggested, my boss loves it, praising how smart it is and then directing me to look into it and work with him on the recommendation.

Inside, I'm livid. I'm brewing with anger. So many thoughts race through my head. About my boss, I silently wonder, *How come he fails to notice my idea, every time? It's ridiculous! He's an idiot!* About my colleague, I think, *Of course! He's the boss's favorite; they always hang out together. He's been schmoozing him since he started to work for him.* Lastly, I turn my anger toward myself. *I can't take this anymore. No one seems to care about me. No one values my work. I feel like a loser here.*

Then my defensive actions follow suit. During the meeting, I am passively defensive, hiding my anger. After the meeting, I often deploy my passive-aggressive defensive actions, gossiping about my boss, putting him down, criticizing him in front of my colleagues, or talking to my team about the poor decisions he makes or how ignorant he is. And once in a while, very rarely, I find myself even behaving aggressively, directly aiming my anger at him, raising my voice, or slamming the door of his office on the way out.

Of course, every time I get triggered like this, I find myself asking whether I want to be here or if I should just quit, move somewhere cheap, and retire. It becomes an internal debate. *But I have good connections here and good friends. I know the system. Maybe I can stay a little longer.* Completely confused, I go home and have a great dinner with my partner, complain about my boss to her, and cool down overnight. I get a good night's sleep and wake up to a new day, my fears and feelings buried inside and forgotten. I go about my work as if nothing happened.

Let's run an internal investigation. I'll start with my thoughts. I had wondered why my boss dismissed my idea but accepted it when a colleague repeated it. My next step would be to challenge this thought with *"what if—so what"* like this:

> Q: What if my boss dismisses my ideas? So
> what?
> A: He always ignores me in meetings. *Try to
> ask* "what if—so what" *again to challenge
> your last thought.*
> Q: What if he ignores me? *Keep turning the
> last thought into a new* "what if" *question.*

> A: I feel my opinions don't matter for him. He
> never listens to what I have to say.
> Q: What if he never listens to me?
> A: I feel not recognized.

Voilà! Here's my repressed fear, the root of everything: the fear of not being recognized. This has been my worst-case scenario since one day long ago, when, after I won a challenging fifteen-hundred-meter track-and-field race, my dad didn't ask anything about it. What made matters worse was that, as time went on, I observed my parents compare my friends to me and praise how smart they were, how well behaved, and so on. By not hearing any positive comments or praise directed at me, I felt not recognized and less-than, thinking and believing I was nobody. There was no interest in what I did, but lots of talk about what others did and what others accomplished. This kind of attitude from my parents made me feel more and more *not recognized*, and I doubted my ability to accomplish anything.

The root, the fear of not being recognized, turned into the cause (i.e., a thought pattern of me not feeling good enough to receive attention or be able to accomplish things). I believed I wasn't anybody of any significance, that whatever I did wasn't going to be seen or praised by others. Finally, the root of not being recognized made me select a set of values that caused me to withdraw from life. I did my own thing without trying to explore beyond what was familiar, fearing that feeling of not being recognized. Why bother to do anything, if I'm not good enough to be recognized for it?

These thoughts, beliefs, and value sets formed the beginning of a limiting life pattern that involved intense self-doubt and self-pity, along with judgmental passive-aggressive defensive actions to push people away and withdraw from people and situations to protect myself from others' lack of interest in me. Those patterns and the underlying repressed fear have been reinforced by limiting life patterns throughout my life since the first days that my parents praised my friends but not me and ignored or dismissed my accomplishments.

Years later, my boss's response to my idea (or lack thereof)—the trigger for this particular limiting life pattern—yet again provoked the repressed fear I'd been carrying within me for decades: the fear that I was not good enough to be recognized, that I would live out my life in misery without accomplishing anything. From a distance, that may sound absurd, but our repressed fears don't need to make sense. They play out the worst-case scenarios in our head. They highlight our worst nightmares. Through my work since then, I have come to understand my fears have affected my perceptions, and the fact that a boss doesn't like my idea doesn't mean I'm not good enough to be recognized or will be forever dismissed and disregarded. Moreover, I've learned that my mom and dad's parenting style didn't mean I was unlovable or not worthy of attention or recognition. They simply didn't want to spoil me with what they deemed excessive praise, and they also wanted to identify some examples of other good behaviors I could adopt, in the hope that I might live my life according to their value system one day.

**Life Skills Assignment #6:
Conduct an internal investigation.**

Expand your daily review practice by incorporating an internal investigation once a week. Choose one of the triggers that repeated frequently throughout that week and OBSERVE the thoughts that were going through your head at the time of the trigger. Then conduct an internal investigation by asking a series of *"what if—so what"* questions to challenge your thoughts until you find your worst-case scenario. Once you identify your repressed fears and understand what it is you're trying to avoid, notice how these repressed fears affect your thoughts and perceptions, and describe how they ignite your emotional reactions when triggered.

> Today's Date: May 4, 2020
> 1. Emotion: I'm anxious.
> 2. Trigger: The girl I'm dating just told me that we'd be better off as friends.
> 3. Thought: I'm shocked. Everything was going so well. She was the perfect one for me. I don't think I'll be able to find anybody like her.
> 4. Repressed Fear: Fear of loneliness.

Does it matter if you found the *right* repressed fear that you've been hiding in your subconscious? No, it doesn't. The most important point here is to find *one* repressed fear every time you conduct an internal investigation, and then to diligently review each repressed fear through different situations to see which ones resonate with you more. The great thing about internal investigation is that there are no right or wrong answers. How others make you feel is very personal—and not negotiable! You'll have plenty of opportunities in life to conduct additional internal investigations as you explore other limiting life patterns and the root of your emotional reactions and defensive actions to triggers.

IMPACT OF REPRESSED FEARS ON LIFE

You've learned how repressed fears color your perceptions, which then initiate your emotional reactions when facing triggers in your limiting life patterns. But on a larger scale, your repressed fears also limit your life experiences, as demonstrated in this "Fleas in a Jar" experiment.

In this experiment, a scientist places a number of fleas in a glass jar. They quickly jump out. He then puts the fleas back into the jar and places a lid over the top. The fleas begin jumping and hitting the lid, falling back down into the jar. After a while, the fleas, conditioned to the presence of the lid, begin jumping less high to avoid hitting it. The scientist then removes the lid and, interestingly enough, the fleas have learned to limit themselves and will not jump higher, even when the lid is not there.

Of course, here the lid represents the boundaries of your comfort zone set by your repressed fears. You feel "safe" under the lid because that's all you know. Your repressed fears of not being good enough, recognized, or valued, for example, keep you in your comfort zone. They hold you back so you can avoid your worst-case scenarios based on your early, painful past experiences. And as long as triggers keep coming back into your life, and your limiting life patterns take charge, you'll give in to your known survival mechanisms and stay in your comfort zone under the lid. Your repressed fears—your sandbags—will continue to dominate your life and hold you down inside your own jar, with heaviness and suffering, until you begin to realize what else is available at higher altitudes of consciousness.

Law of Life #7:
The higher you are on the scale of consciousness, the freer you'll be in life.

Now you start to see the deep and strong correlation between your personal freedom, your repressed fears, and your level of consciousness. Whether you are high or low on the scale of consciousness is not a source of self-judgment, but an inspiration for self-empowerment. Knowing your level, and owning it, will help you understand and process the sandbags that hold you at that particular level. Any denial, judgment, or attempt to escape without taking ownership of your consciousness level will be defensive and therefore a wasted effort—the sandbags remain unprocessed, and actions like this will eventually pull you down. Therefore, the question you'll be exploring next is what consciousness level you are at today, and what kind of sandbags, or repressed fears, hold you down at that level.

UNDERSTANDING YOUR REPRESSED FEARS

You've been running away from your vulnerability all your life. You now know why you emotionally react to triggers. You've begun to identify the cycle of your own limiting life patterns. You've started to think about the root-cause-effect relationships, and now the time has come to face your repressed fears and, ultimately, break free from that vicious cycle. This next step is all about why you've been on guard for so long, feeling stuck, lost, and confused. It's time to further decode your survival mechanisms, driven by your subconscious internal programming, and uncover the root of all that happens to you in life.

Let's review some hypothetical limiting life pattern cycles surrounding commonly repressed fears. First we'll explore the triggers, then the perceptions coloring those triggers, and finally the possible origin of those perceptions (i.e., the initial incidents that gave birth to your repressed fears).

Fear of Not Being Good Enough

Trigger: Your partner criticizes whatever you do: the way you load the dishwasher, the way you talk when you hang out with your friends, the way you dress, the type of friends you have, the way you interact with others, and maybe even your opinions. You always want to do things perfectly, orderly, and neatly, yet your partner always has something to say about you, some form of criticism that puts you down.

Perception: You are never good enough for anyone or at anything.

Origins: Maybe, growing up, you had very strict parents: your dad was a disciplinarian, and your mom was controlling. You were not allowed to make mistakes. Everything you did was closely monitored. You only received brief praise, followed by further instructions on how to be better.

Fear of Not Being Recognized

Trigger: A colleague is promoted to a position that you feel you deserved. You work hard at your job, take pride in what you do, and had been talking to your boss about this possible promotion for months. On another occasion, your boss sends a group email to all the vice presidents and takes credit for work you've done.

Perception: You are never recognized by others.

Origins: Maybe, as you were growing up, your dad was distant and aloof, and he didn't care about your accomplishments or other aspects of your life. Your mom was also emotionally unavailable and never saw you for who you were.

Fear of Abandonment

Trigger: Your husband has started hanging out with his buddies more and staying at work longer. In fact, he missed the dinner date that both of you had planned for the other night. He also seems to exchange personal texts and emails with a female colleague who is not on his team. He doesn't want to hang out with you as much or do the things that you both used to enjoy doing together.

Perception: Anyone can abruptly distance themselves from you, or even leave you, at any time, without notice.

Origins: Maybe, when you were in seventh grade or so, your mom forgot to pick you up from school one day. She was only an hour late when she arrived, but you were the only one waiting in the schoolyard. Or maybe your parents got divorced when you were a child, and one of them took off, and you never saw that parent again until after you'd grown up. Or maybe, when you were at college, the boy or girl you were madly in love with suddenly left you for another person.

Fear of Loneliness

Trigger: You feel empty after another big party you organized. All of your friends already left. You are sitting on your couch in your living room, ruminating about the night and the interactions you had with your friends. Even though they're a great group of friends, the connections aren't as close as you'd like.

Perception: There's nobody out there that you can deeply and intimately connect with.

Origins: Maybe your parents were very loving and caring while you were growing up. They organized playdates and birthday parties for you. You became very social. You were always the center of friendship cliques. You relied on the warmth and support your parents provided over the years, but were never able to reconstruct that kind of deep connection with others. So you keep forming a lot of friendships, trying to find such intimacy, without much luck.

Fear of Failure

Trigger: You are about to launch a business venture, yet you feel overwhelmed by the amount of work you need to put in, and by negative self-talk about how you can't possibly get your idea going, so you keep procrastinating a little longer, waiting to push your venture forward.

Perception: You can't excel at anything due to your mediocre, ordinary nature.

Origins: Maybe, while you were growing up, your parents always thought you were an OK kid, but there was nothing special about you. They weren't ambitious types; they never grabbed life by its horns. They let you do whatever you wanted, but without guiding you how to be better, how to succeed. You also thought of yourself as a mediocre student at school, standing on the sidelines as other kids were actively involved in projects and clubs, earning lots of glory and praise and awards.

Fear of Betrayal

Trigger: At dinner with another couple, your wife starts to chat with the other husband about how much they enjoy playing tennis and whether they should get together one day for a game or two. They are so excited about their mutual interest that you feel left out. You suspect they may like each other, and tennis is an excuse to spend time together.

Perception: You can't rely on anyone to stand by you. No one is trustworthy.

Origins: Your parents may have preferred to work or spend time with their own friends, rather than spend time with you.

Fear of Not Being Valued

Trigger: Yet again, your partner doesn't seem to understand all that you do for family. Also, your desire for intimacy isn't reciprocated anymore.

Perception: Nobody sees you and you don't have any worth or value in this world.

Origins: Your parents may have been so busy with work or parental obligations that they didn't pay much attention to you. Or you may have even been raised by an older sibling.

Fear of Rejection

Trigger: Your partner no longer seems interested in your ideas.

Perception: People don't care about you or your needs.

Origins: Your parents may have encouraged you to pursue interests that satisfied their own needs and desires rather than yours.

Fear of Dismissal

Trigger: You recently offered help to someone in need and didn't even receive a thank you. When you need help, no one shows up.

Perception: You need to attend to others' needs before your own.

Origins: Even though you worked hard at home to make your parents happy, they never appreciated your efforts and ignored your needs for emotional intimacy. They spent more time with your older sister. You kept helping them in the hope that one day they'd see you and appreciate your efforts.

Fear of Inadequacy

Trigger: Your popular and successful partner is on yet another business trip. They're always on the go these days, while you're back at home waiting for their return.

Perceptions: You don't have your own intrinsic value. Also, other people use you.

Origins: Your parents may have been self-absorbed and expected you to accommodate their needs. They were quick to criticize when your service to them fell short of their expectations.

Fear of Success, or "Imposter Syndrome"

Trigger: Although you're very accomplished in your professional and personal life, you become anxious whenever attention is directed at you.

Perception: People will, one day, discover you aren't nearly as smart, polished, or talented as you appear. They'll wonder how you got to where you are today.

Origins: Your parents may not have recognized your value or achievements, no matter how successful you were, while you were growing up. They failed to see who you were, so you keep trying to prove yourself to them.

Fear of Not Being Approved

Trigger: You ask people's opinions all the time, even on the simplest decisions, like what to have for dinner. On another night, you're frustrated by your indecision on what to cook. You're often intimidated by your partner and by your parents, who expect you to behave in a certain way, and you feel like you have to explain your actions. You often find yourself saying "I'm sorry" to avoid upsetting others.

Perception: You'll be criticized, put down, ridiculed, ousted, and maybe even shunned for making the wrong decisions.

Origins: Your parents may have been very strict and controlling, perpetually disappointed in you if they didn't agree with the choices you made.

Fear of Missing Out

Trigger: You saw another friend post their fun vacation on social media. You hate this sense of stagnancy and become jealous of others when they experience life more than you do.

Perception: Life is meant to be lived through experiences that will make you more valuable, popular, and interesting. Everyone seems to have more fun than you do.

Origins: Your family life may have been dull and mundane, and the exciting and fun life experiences always happened to everyone else, outside your window.

Fear of Judgment

Trigger: You're stressed about hosting your parents-in-law for the weekend because they're so critical and meticulous.

Perception: People are out to get you and critically scrutinize everything you do.

Origins: Your parents or teachers may have pressured you to perform at a certain level that you felt was unachievable, and when you missed the mark, you were scolded or mocked.

Fear of Financial Instability

Trigger: You lose a significant contract with a major customer. You fail at an important job interview. You are let go from your current job. You are in the process of getting divorced.

Perception: Financial resources can be taken away from you.

Origins: Your family may have experienced financial hardships while you were growing up, and as a result you were deprived of things you wanted. You came to believe that life is full of surprises and nothing is certain.

Do any of these repressed fears and life experiences resonate with you? Do any of them show up frequently as part of your limiting life patterns? Studying your repressed fears and their origins may be daunting, yet it is an essential task to rise in consciousness. You may discover things about your Self that bring up unpleasant memories, old regrets, and painful experiences for you to process.

If you feel triggered during this process, please remember this: You are not alone. We are all in this together. Everyone has their story. No one is immune to repressed fears. A trigger is a messenger that provokes your repressed fears as an invitation to discover them, to deal with them, to understand their origins, and finally, to grow out of them.

Also, your life story is completely unique to you, and when you observe your thoughts and trace them back to repressed fears and to their origins, you discover important elements of your own story. Through this exploration, and through acceptance of your repressed fears and of the life experiences that created them, you slowly take power back into your hands and away from the reign of your subconscious internal programming. This newly acquired inner skill will help you break free from the limiting life patterns that prevent you from living at your highest potential, Ultimate Happiness.

Law of Life #8:
Understanding your repressed fears leads you to acceptance of your vulnerability.

Identifying the origin of your repressed fears, and understanding what really took place during those initial life experiences, will help you decode your subconscious survival mechanisms and deepen your journey of self-discovery.

Life Skills Assignment #7:
Review early memories that may be the origin of your repressed fears.

As part of your daily review, can you reflect on your previous life experiences to discover the earliest incidents, the origins that may have formed your repressed fears?

Today's Date: September 22, 2020
1. Emotion: Angry, sad.
2. Trigger: Latest news, social media feeds, people's attitudes toward each other.
3. Thought: There is so much injustice and unfairness in the world. I see conflict everywhere, and so many people are depressed, unhappy, and anxious.

4. Repressed Fear: Fear of conflict, being judged, being bullied.

5. Origins: Growing up, I witnessed my parents fight a lot. My dad drank a lot and had a short temper. He was very critical of my mom's actions and often unexpectedly raised his voice at her and at me for petty reasons, creating chaos and conflict at home. I wanted to stand up and protect my mom, but never did. I didn't want to escalate the arguments. Instead, I attended to chores around the house in an attempt to make her life easier. As a result, I learned to be conflict-averse, yet very empathetic to the suffering and emotional pain of others, often redirecting my anger and sadness to the injustice and abuse in the world.

Note that you don't have to find the very first incident, but try to go back as early as you can. In doing so, you may become stressed out. If you feel the pain of those days, of those years, try not to identify yourself with the experience. You can do this by using self-observation, as you learned to do with the self-observation meditation technique: Step back and become an objective observer, an outside witness of your Self, and remember that your perceptions today are only a web of thought patterns and belief systems based on your repressed fears, which are the outcome of your prior experiences.

As we discussed earlier, your subconscious internal programming gives your life its meaning, but until you truly understand that programming—with all the repressed fears and related perceptions—you may have difficulty knowing how to manage or interpret your life experiences, someone else's actions, others' attitudes, or challenging situations. When you gain a deeper understanding of your repressed fears, you gain access to self-knowledge about why you emotionally react. As a result, you can manage your defensive actions more effectively and preserve some of that energy you usually spent defending your vulnerability. With more knowledge about your Self and more energy stored in your body, your sandbags naturally become lighter and lighter, allowing you to rise up above limiting life patterns. That's why taking the time to PAUSE and OBSERVE is so important on our journey toward Ultimate Happiness.

Life genuinely wants you to destroy the thick walls of your comfort zone, fully embrace your highest potential, and experience the Ultimate Happiness you came here to experience. Until now, your repressed fears have governed your life. But now the time has come for you to learn to live with your repressed fears as part of your Truth—as you identify them, name them, and understand them—and not to be controlled by them.

CHAPTER FOUR

WELCOMING WHAT'S ARISING IN YOUR BODY

What do you think might have happened to you as a child if you brought home a B- for a difficult subject, but were scolded by your parents because you didn't get an A?

You would've probably felt ashamed, not good enough, belittled, put down.

But what might have happened afterward? What would you have done with those feelings?

You couldn't possibly express them to your parents because they seemed so intimidating. And, as a kid, you didn't know how to process these feelings either. Even as adults, we often don't know how. So you buried them. Your emotional pain was so hurtful to deal with, and so painful to process, you stored it away to hide your vulnerability, which then became the repressed fears that you started to carry around as sandbags into the future.

Where do you think you buried these feelings of shame and belittlement, of not being good enough, of being put down?

In your body.

Looking back to my childhood, to a story similar to the one above, I distinctly remember my dad's words: *Speak when you have something smart to say.* In retrospect, I don't know if he meant to say that I was a smart kid and I should use my words wisely, or that I was talking nonsense and he wanted me to shut up. Regardless, this "uttering only smart words" was an important life tenet for him, part of his value set, and he wanted me to follow in his footsteps.

But when I heard him say this phrase, at fourteen, my face turned red, and I had a fiery sensation in the pit of my stomach. That's exactly where I recorded the incident—in my stomach, storing my vulnerability about not being smart, not having anything worthwhile to say, not being valued, not having a voice. And since then, every time I've spoken in a group or even met a new person, and all of the attention was directed at me, my face turned red. Sweat flashed over me. My voice weakened. And a cramp formed in the pit of my stomach, the way one did the first time he said those words.

I invite you to reflect back on your own youth and try to recall a time when you were emotionally hurt. Do you remember the sensations your body had at that traumatic moment? What about similar incidents that repeated throughout your adolescence that also registered in your body?

Now ask yourself this: When you feel triggered, does your body tense up, tighten, contract, and feel heavy or depleted, as if you were facing exactly those same situations from your youth?

What's going on here?

Those physical sensations that you felt back then are resurfacing because the triggers, as the messengers of your sandbags, are activating your repressed fears again. We already know the triggers remind your subconscious about that emotional pain, but they also provoke your body to realize how much vulnerability hurts. So your body takes on a defensive stance. And every time it does—that is, every time you react without being aware of your repressed fears or understanding what's beneath your emotional reactions—you're essentially adding more sand to your sandbags. Of course, over time, they get heavier and heavier, eventually pulling you down.

No matter how high your balloon rises, sooner or later, someone makes a remark or does something that triggers you and drags you back down to choppy and unhappy lower altitudes, where you invoke yet another limiting life pattern cycle. You emotionally react to fight back against the trigger, and when you do, you end up depleting your energy and sliding back into another state of conflict and confusion. And all the while the trigger is trying to alert you, invite you to look for your repressed fears so they are revealed and eventually released once and for all.

Only a James Bond movie can explain this crazy phenomenon. In one of them, our beloved Agent 007 goes to a casino in Monaco to spy on the bad guys. But they know who 007 is, and they play a little trick on him. They plant a microchip in his pocket when he's distracted by his beautiful companion and his "shaken, not stirred" martini. When Bond leaves the casino and jumps into his latest-series BMW, the bad guys fire the missile rocket that tracks the microchip, and we viewers become enthralled by a high-speed chase through the streets of Monaco. Of course, Bond ultimately discovers the microchip in his pocket, just as his tires screech around a dangerous curve, and he throws it out the window over a cliff. The missile explodes, and Bond speeds off to his villa in the French Riviera.

In my story, my father could be considered the bad guy, although he wasn't an actual villain and didn't mean to hurt me. Instead of planting a microchip in my pocket, he planted a repressed fear inside my body—in my stomach. But whereas Bond found the microchip just in time, I didn't find my fear.

Triggers have chased me through life like missiles, exploding over and over again. And each time, the whole limiting life pattern cycle repeated, provoking my emotions and upsetting my stomach, until my energy reserves were depleted and I was left feeling stuck, lost, and confused.

The repressed fears you carry in your body are also like that dangerous microchip. Bond may not have seemed terribly frightened when he found that device, but unearthing your repressed fears can be painful, which is of course why you buried them in the first place. You may not want to look at them or even know about them. You may not want to go back to the memories and experiences that formed these repressed fears. It's much easier to blame the missiles, or triggers: the situations, the kids, the parents, and so on. Yet life's invitation remains steadfast: *Please find your microchip. Release your sandbags. Rise above your limiting life patterns. Realize your highest potential. Experience your Ultimate Happiness!*

Law of Life #9:
You keep reliving your past through the repressed fears buried in your body.

Why do you need to find out what's buried?

Imagine sandbags are hidden in various parts of your body: in your stomach, across your shoulders, beneath your heart, and so on. One, they feel heavy. Two, those parts of your body are locked up, tense, excluded, denied, ignored, not recognized, not acknowledged. That means a big part of you isn't integrated with the rest of your self; your mental, emotional, and physical components aren't operating in unison. Some parts of you are out of balance, out of alignment—or maybe even not functioning. That means you are not whole. You are not complete. You are not one hundred percent you!

What does it mean to not be aligned or integrated at the mental, emotional, and physical layers of Self? Let's explore this question by looking at how my dad's words, *"speak when you have something smart to say,"* contributed to a disintegration of my Self. Picture me in a group of cheery, talkative people. Something interesting comes to my mind that I want to share. But then self-talk filters in. *Don't say anything right now. It's not a smart thing to say. Don't look stupid. What do you know about this anyway? You're not that smart.*

While this inner dialogue happens in my head, my heart wants me to share. I want to impress or have a deep conversation with my friends in the group. I want to connect with them. So now I'm really torn. To which voice should I listen? While this conflict is going on between my mind and heart, my body begins to suffer. My shoulders hunch; my stomach churns. I can feel my face reddening, and I start to sweat.

This supposedly fun social interaction, with everyone talking cheerfully, turns into a limiting life pattern and triggers me. I become anxious quickly and don't know what to do. I have no idea how to get into conversations. All layers of my Self seem to point in different directions, toward different choices. I could talk about something intellectual. I could make small talk. I could crack a joke. At the same time, I don't want to interrupt anyone. Maybe I should stay quiet. What shall I do? It feels as if my right foot is on the gas pedal, and my left is on the brake. My heart wants to join in the fun, take action, drive forward. But my head is afraid and has no idea where to go. I'm about to explode, while at the same time I'm starting to feel too tired to say anything at all. My stomach is, by now, a mess, and my whole body is stiffening. I feel paralyzed, so debilitated that I doubt I can even make a noise or speak a word. So I deploy my usual passive defensive action and withdraw. I stand there quietly. I shy away from being noticed at all. Moments pass, and soon I begin to chastise myself because I didn't share what I wanted to share. And then I realize I have landed in that familiar state of conflict and confusion. I try to collect myself and let everything cool down. Sometimes, that cool down and collection process can take only a few minutes and I can rejoin the fun, but other times it takes a while, maybe hours or days, and I carry my negative inner chatter to bed with me, affecting my sleep, or even wake up with it, which ruins my mood for the day.

Another example of not being fully integrated may be seen in overeating. In this case, your mind wants to control your eating because it thinks it's unhealthy. You may have even gained a few pounds recently, which you want to shed before attending an upcoming social event. But your heart isn't going along with the plan. Maybe it encourages you to eat because you're bored at home or at work. Or you've been stressed out lately. Or you deserve a reward for your recent hard work, so you indulge in pumpkin pie, chocolate chip cookies, ice cream, popcorn, or candies. Eating comfort or junk food can be like going on vacation. It's fun, and we all need fun in our lives. But it can also become a battle between your mind and your heart, which can in itself serve as a trigger that leads to physical tension, which leads to agitation, which leads to confusion and conflict about why you don't have control over your eating habits.

In another situation, you might be at work, putting in long hours. Your mind wants you to work because you like it, and you also want to get promoted, be recognized, or maybe earn a raise. On the other hand, your heart wants to have dinner with the family, explore a new part of the city, practice your guitar, or go home and read a book over a glass of wine with soft piano music in the background. When you pause to evaluate your body, you notice how tight your shoulders are. In fact, your entire body is tense and stressed. The internal conflict has triggered you, and your chosen defensive action, this time, is to stay late and work. But when you finally arrive home, you can't calm your mind down even though your body is exhausted. And that means you wake up tired. You consider going into work late, but you know that's not a good idea, and now you find yourself having slipped into that state of internal conflict and confusion as you wonder what you should do next.

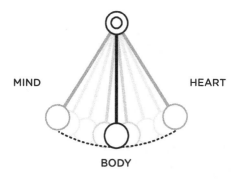

Like a pendulum, you keep swinging between your mind and heart as they pull you in different directions, causing you to feel debilitated and paralyzed. When your mind and heart work against each other like that, you need a third element, a third component to bring them together, to melt them into each other so you can center yourself and align the different layers of your Self. That third element is your body. However, when your body has repressed fears buried within, it doesn't have the capacity to resolve this kind of internal conflict between your mind and heart. That's why you need to find out what's buried in your body first so you can cleanse, clear out what's holding you back, and then build toward being one hundred percent You, one hundred percent Real—in other words, fully integrated in all of the actions, performances, and relationships in your life.

DROPPING INTO THE BODY

The body can definitely help reconcile the internal conflict between the mind and the heart. It can be the container to integrate them. However, before this integration takes place, we need to drop into the body and identify the sandbags, clear the turf, and cleanse the container, so the body can hold space for this integration. Then it can help lift you toward higher consciousness. This cleansing process is called *digestion of sandbags*.

This digestion process is how you will work with, and ultimately release, your sandbags. First by noticing them, then breaking them down into workable pieces, then slowly absorbing them into the body, and ultimately eliminating them altogether. This process can also be likened to two heavy millstones slowly and patiently grinding the grain into flour, symbolizing the arduous and painful process of eliminating old wounds and ego structures and opening the space, the body, for rebirth through transformation of consciousness.

This process begins with the third step in the POWER Method, which is WELCOME. This step is all about acknowledging the physical sensations the triggers provoke in your body as places where your repressed fears lie buried.

Remember that the POWER Method is about breaking free from your limiting life pattern cycle. The first step, PAUSE, comes into play when you first notice your emotional reactions to a trigger. OBSERVE then asks you, in the first phase, to observe your thoughts before you deploy your defensive actions. The second phase of OBSERVE invites you to acknowledge the physical sensations arising in your body. When you are able to acknowledge what's happening, you are preparing to accept it, and then even WELCOME it. Similar to the beginning of any digestion process, you acknowledge the food before you chew and swallow it. Then you take it into your body as a sign of your acceptance of the food, and you digest it as the food becomes absorbed by the cells of your body as nutrition. This is very similar to digesting sandbags—every repressed fear, every part of your body that is ignored, becomes acknowledged and reclaimed, as if puzzle pieces come together to give you the full picture of who you really are!

This journey of self-discovery leads to what ancient traditions call Self-Realization. By discovering parts of your Self, by digesting your repressed fears, and by identifying layers of your comfort zone, you reveal your Real Self. You don't need to go to monasteries for self-discovery; life happens right in front of you and gives you plenty of opportunities to examine and observe. You don't need to sit for hours on top of a mountain to reflect on your inner workings and know who you are. Life is your mirror, and you can use its reflections for your revelations. Your quest for Self-Realization doesn't even have to be spiritual, religious, or agnostic. Your own life is a lab for your experiments, and your own experiences are the evidence that guides you to your Real Self.

Right here. Right now. You can become your Real Self—your highest potential—and realize Ultimate Happiness.

Law of Life #10:
The golden key that opens the doors to Ultimate Happiness is locked inside your body.

What does the act of *welcoming a physical sensation* mean?

Imagine one of your least favorite friends is knocking at your door. It's a surprise visit. She was driving by your neighborhood and decided to drop by. What do you do? Do you ignore her and pretend you are not at home?

Welcoming the physical sensation means sitting with your repressed fears, not running away from them. Your friend at the door has always been judgmental toward you in the past, and you've always felt bad about yourself when you've been with her. Your perception is that, if you invite her in, she's going to put you down again, provoking your repressed fears of not being valued, being misunderstood, being judged, or being less-than. Ordinarily, you'd push her away as a defensive action. But instead, this time, you want to digest your sandbags. You want to face your repressed fears. So you open the door, invite her in, and ask her to find a comfortable spot in your living room. You offer her a cup of tea and maybe even a freshly baked chocolate chip cookie. Or a glass of fine wine that you keep for special occasions. You sit down with your unwanted guest. You listen to what she has to say. Of course, it's going to be very uncomfortable to be next to her, but you don't push her away. Your new goal is to understand her a little better, to be curious about who she is, and to listen to what she has to share.

By inviting her in, you honor your repressed fears instead of running away from them. You also honor their physical sensations: pain, tension, and contraction. WELCOME is all about acknowledging those physical sensations. I call this step *conscious discomfort.* You basically sit with whatever physical sensation arises in your body, without trying to patch or cover it up with positive thoughts, and without numbing it with mantras and chants and lalalalala screams. You are simply there, sitting with it!

It's the most difficult act, yet also the most powerful. We talked about this before, and it's worth mentioning here again. Your subconscious internal programming is, in essence, a code that has been written by your repressed fears. It determines your thought patterns, belief systems, and value sets. It colors your perceptions. It causes you to emotionally react to triggers.

Yes, triggers are real. There will always be difficult people and challenging situations. But your perception of reality no longer needs to be biased by your repressed fears.

WELCOME, the act of conscious discomfort, is not about suddenly breaking down or destroying or eliminating these repressed fears. They are integral parts of your survival mechanisms, and they provide a valuable reference point for how to live, how to survive. Conscious discomfort is, instead, about taking power away from your repressed fears. It is about returning the power to your own hands, using it in your own conscious decision-making process, and learning to discern, without the influence of your repressed fears, which actions are appropriate. Conscious discomfort is, in essence, a face-off against your repressed fears.

The question to ask yourself now is this: Do you have the fabric, the stamina, to be the hero of your self-discovery journey?

In *The Hero with a Thousand Faces*, Joseph Campbell unpacked the details of the traditional hero's journey as found in most mythological narratives. A hero is a character who dares to undertake a journey of individual freedom and discovery, hoping to eventually realize their highest potential. The typical template for this hero's journey is a common narrative in which the individual leaves their ordinary life, goes on an adventure, embarks on a difficult journey that usually involves physical pain as well as emotional discomfort, learns their lessons, wins victories against all odds, and then returns home transformed. They're now self-assured due to the knowledge of Self and Life that they gained along their journey.

For centuries, these myths have been inviting us to narrate our own stories, in which we transition from the heaviness of subconscious internal programming to the lightness of being our Real Self. Like the hero, you, too, can rise above the ordinary and move toward higher levels of consciousness to realize your destiny, your highest potential, your Ultimate Happiness.

What might your story look like?

Let's say you've been comfortably living in your village, within the tight confines of your comfort zone—according to your internal programming, as created by your repressed fears. You know most of the people in the village. You follow the common routines. You know how to get by from day to day. Yet every day is the same: the same conversations, the same routines. Initially, what you thought was comfortable now makes you feel stuck. The daily routines have become stagnant and boring. Confusion starts to settle in. You might even start to wonder about moving to a different, maybe better, life beyond your village.

Interestingly enough, everyone intuitively knows about this different life. They whisper about its beauty and magic among friends and behind closed doors. Yet no one has ever dared to venture away from the village because of the dragon who lives in the forest. As long as the villagers stay put, the dragon doesn't bother them, even protecting them from outside threats. The villagers have accepted these living conditions for centuries because they're safe, even if their individual freedoms are restricted.

Except you! You begin to envision how you might face off with the dragon. The question is: Can you endure the discomfort and pain necessary to venture through the forest and beyond, in search of this higher life? Can you leave the contracted boundaries of your comfort zone? Can you explore the unknown and embrace the uncertainty?

The dragon represents the repressed fears that hold you in your comfort zone. When you live within the security of your village, and the confines of your comfort zone, you can easily ignore your vulnerability. In your head, because you have done everything possible to repress your fears and form a comfortable life, you think that *life is safe and secure*—until a limiting life pattern rears up with a trigger. As you have experienced, the corresponding pain ignites your defensive actions and your attention goes outward, to the trigger. After exhausting yourself through various defensive actions, you lose your power to the trigger. And the limiting life pattern cycle continues—the cycle that makes you feel stuck.

As a result, the trigger becomes a distraction that pulls your attention away from your inner work. That's why your self-observation meditation is so important—it builds the muscle of your attention and helps you stay focused despite the distraction of outside stimulus—in this case, your triggers. The dragon is not your triggers. Triggers are still the invitations, the messengers that direct you to your sandbags. However, because you've been so occupied defending yourself against the outside triggers you've been blaming for your unhappiness, you managed to avoid the internal fight; in other words, you managed to avoid the digestion process, the dragon, and the repressed fears that lie within you. You've been avoiding this fight for a good reason: it's painful and scary, and it pushes against your comfort zone.

If, instead of reacting, you choose to respond to these triggers by going inward, by welcoming the fight against the dragon, by facing your repressed fears, you will start to grind up and digest the sandbags that hold you in lower consciousness levels, in intense and frequent limiting life patterns. You will start to slowly rise above the matrix, above the house of cards, above your comfort zone, and ultimately achieve the higher consciousness levels where you realize Ultimate Happiness.

Law of Life #11:
Facing the pain of your vulnerability is the eye of the needle you pass through for Self-Realization.

Turning inward is a fundamental part of WELCOME, which is all about the process of digesting the sandbags. You basically welcome the emotional charges that show up as physical sensations in your body as a result of a trigger. You may feel these charges in the pit of your stomach when your partner criticizes you; as tension headaches after a long, stressful day filled with challenges from your colleagues; as heaviness in your chest when you're sad about your parents growing old. They show up in the form of pressure across your shoulders when you feel anxious and worried about paying the bills. They are the pins and needles all over your skin when you walk into a party and don't know anyone.

When you apply the POWER Method, you always start with PAUSE, so that you can slow things down and notice your emotions. Then you OBSERVE your thoughts and the physical sensations in your body. You are now at the next step: WELCOME. How can you welcome this kind of discomfort, this kind of pain, when you're triggered?

You start by simply sitting with the pain, consciously experiencing the discomfort, the tension, the contraction, or whatever else you may be feeling in your body at the time.

Why do you need to sit with the pain of your repressed fears?

Law of Life # 12:
Because everything is stored in the body, everything needs to be processed and digested in the body.

Going back to our digestion process analogy, sitting with the emotional pain as you face your repressed fears feels exactly like trying to process a big, heavy meal. Picture that very first incident, the traumatic event that created your repressed fear, as a big meal. You ate it, but you couldn't digest it immediately. It was too heavy. You had to let your body slowly break it down, piece by piece.

Until you can properly process the emotional impact of that triggering situation, it stays stored within your body, like a heavy meal, including all the pain and the related thought patterns, belief systems, and value sets. It imprints onto your subconscious internal programming and, over time, becomes a repressed fear, a sandbag in your body. And just as the original heavy meal can leave a bitter taste in your mouth, a bitterness arises inside your body every time you face a similar situation, triggering similar emotional reactions.

Fortunately, your digestive systems eventually process the food and you don't have to keep it inside forever. Your repressed fears, however, remain buried in your body and could stay there unprocessed for years, sometimes manifesting as illness and chronic pain. The good news is that Life *wants* you to process, and digest, the buried fears from the past. Through the limiting life patterns, as reminders of what you need to work on, Life extends the invitation to you to work on your personal and spiritual growth. It sends triggers to help you cleanse your body, integrate your mind and heart, and eventually experience Ultimate Happiness.

Law of Life #13:
Triggers only exist because of repressed fears.

Since you have been granted the invitation to digest your repressed fears through the triggers, let's look at how you can use each limiting life pattern to do this.

DIGESTING REPRESSED FEARS

When you repressed a fear in the original incident of your past, your subconscious figured you wouldn't want to experience that vulnerability again. So your internal programming hid this repressed fear inside a steel vault and threw the key into the river, where no one would be able to find it. The vault has remained stored in your body for years, but now it's time to open it up, WELCOME your physical discomfort, and digest your fears.

> **Life Skills Assignment #8:**
> **Drop into your body to face**
> **your vulnerability.**

At least once a day, notice your emotional reaction to a trigger and trace its charge within your body. Where does the emotional charge show up? Notice the specific physical sensations. At the end of the day, write down your observations as part of your daily review.

While describing your observation, try to be imaginative. Start by assessing its intensity on a scale of 1 to 10, with 10 being very intense, heavy, and painful. Get closer to it if you can, sitting with it for a while. Take a look at it from outside, as a detached observer. How might you describe the size of this physical sensation? Its shape? Color? Texture? Can you describe it using a metaphor—is it a tennis ball, an orange, a fluid, a heavy rock, a watermelon? Here's an example of a daily review entry for your reference:

> Today's Date: October 19, 2020
> 1. Emotion: Overwhelmed.
> 2. Trigger: Too many things on my plate.
> 3. Thought: Can't handle it anymore. Want to run away.

Now, for step four, conduct your internal investigation starting from your thoughts all the way down to your repressed fears using the *"what if—so what"* methodology.

> 4. Repressed Fear: What if I can't handle it anymore? *People will judge me.* What if people judge me? *I will look bad in front them.* What if I look bad? *They'll think I'm not good enough—not adequate—to handle these things.* Repressed Fear: Not good enough—or fear of being inadequate.
> 5. Origins: Looking back and reflecting on my life growing up, I realized that my dad praised me so highly and expected so much from me that, in order to please

him, or at least not disappoint him, I was
involved in lots of extracurricular activities during middle school and high school,
even to some degree at college. I loved
getting involved. I was proud of all my
accomplishments. And I knew that my dad
was proud of me, too, thus validating me.
But now I have a family, a demanding job,
and two busy kids. I have so much to do:
driving them to school activities, attending to family needs, trying to meet up
with friends, running errands that never
seem to end. I'm completely overwhelmed.
Origins: Doing it all to meet my dad's
expectations.

Now it's time to drop into your body to discover where you
feel the emotional charge of being overwhelmed as a physical
sensation. You do this through self-observation. But instead
of using your thumbs in the self-observation meditation practice, you turn your focus inward to your body. You maintain a
detached observer state to look at what's going on in your body.
Then you tune into the emotional charge that you experience,
connecting with the physical sensations your emotions create.

Can you feel it? If so, where is it? If not, don't worry for now.
Since we all live in our heads and rarely connect with our bodies, it may be difficult in the beginning to sense the emotional
charge as a physical sensation in the body. Take your time. Sit
down and observe your thoughts. Then try to softly scan your
body with an inner gaze to see if you can detect any noticeable physical sensations, like tightness in your upper chest, or
a lump in your throat, or the hint of a punch in your gut.

6. Body Part: After sitting quietly for a few minutes, I started scanning my body and came across some sensations in my upper chest. It was subtle at first. When I focused on it, it became more palpable. I then realized that it was related to the emotional charge of being overwhelmed. Body Part: Upper chest.

Now describe it. What is its intensity, on that scale of 1 to 10? What is its size, shape, and color? Keep going as deep as you can, noticing as you explore how, or if, the physical sensations shift.

7. Sensation: As I tuned into the physical sensation in my upper chest, I sensed its intensity as high. I would say around an 8. It was like a very heavy tennis ball. Its color was brown. Due to the heaviness, it felt like a contraction in my chest. I almost felt like this heaviness wanted to scream out loud: *Enough already!* Sensation: Heaviness pressing into upper chest. Intensity of 8. Tennis-ball shape. Brown color. Suffocating feeling.

Finally, it's time to practice conscious discomfort. Close your eyes and try to sit with these physical sensations that have arisen in your body, maybe for ten or twenty or even thirty seconds (yes, seconds, not minutes). See how that feels for you, but if it's too much, that's OK. There's no pressure here, so if you don't feel ready, don't do it just yet. Be patient with this process, and stay with what you *are* ready to accept at this point. Once you are more familiar and experienced, you may be able to sit with uncomfortable physical sensations up to five minutes each time. For now, try to stay present with the pain and discomfort that you feel in your body.

You may be wondering why you need to recall the day's emotional pain and sit with it during your daily review. The reason is the hurt that the trigger caused within you does not go away when you get over your emotional reactions and move on to other things. That emotional pain is still there, stored in your body, in that same sandbag where your repressed fears are stored. Therefore, there's no good or bad time to practice conscious discomfort. When you want to process your repressed fears and digest your sandbags, it's best to do it when the memory of a limiting life pattern is fresh, so you can bring up the emotions as vividly as possible and gain access to the deepest levels of your repressed fears with the highest emotional pain, reaching to intensity levels of 7 and above. With that emotional pain comes the opportunity to sit with your repressed fears and slowly grind through them, instead of running away and leaving them stored in your body.

Law of Life #14:
The only way out is through.

Life keeps provoking the emotional pain stored in your body so you can face it, not run away from it. If you do choose to ignore the invitation, you now know that you will keep running into the same triggers that previously made you feel the same way, basically keeping you in the hamster wheel, in circles. You need to slowly and painfully walk through your current level of consciousness, as if through thick mud, and patiently sit with the emotional pain, before you can expect to experience a higher level of consciousness.

EXPERIENCING CONSCIOUSNESS SHIFT

When you sit with your physical sensations and WELCOME your repressed fears, you start to experience the pain that your body has been holding in for years. Everything you repressed at that very first traumatic incident—the painful memories, the unexpressed hurt, the unspoken feelings, the unprocessed trauma—may come out from the previously secure vault within your body.

However, this time, you don't run away. You turn inward and face the original hurt right there in your body. You stay there and face the dragon against all odds—face your repressed fears despite all that pain. And then you slowly begin to move forward, through the pain, through the conscious discomfort, one step at a time. It may seem like a dance with your dragon: a lunge forward, a step back, and then another lunge forward. You advance toward your adversary through the forest, not around it.

And yes, it is with both fright and hope that you walk step-by-step through the forest. With each step, you slowly discover the power shifting back into your hands, back to your Real Self. Your repressed fears are loosening up. They're getting ready to be released, freed from your body. You get a sense that you may no longer be stuck in the limiting life pattern cycles. And you start to feel that you have risen to a higher level of consciousness that allows you to respond differently to the triggers you'll encounter in the future.

Law of Life #15:
When you face what you fear, the
balance of power shifts to you.

When you start to take your power back from the triggers, you also take it back from the people or situations that have caused you pain or frightened you. You start rebuilding your inner strength—that presence we discussed earlier—and you begin to stand up for your Self. You reclaim your individual freedom; you break away from whatever holds you back or holds you down. You let go of whatever has been keeping you in the lower altitudes of suffering.

I remember experiencing excruciatingly painful moments when I practiced conscious discomfort. On one of those occasions, I was sitting on the side of my bed all alone. It was Saturday night. I had no friend to call, no date to go on, no family nearby. It had been only one week since I had broken up from a long-term relationship that meant the world to me. As I faced my emptiness, I looked at the possibility of never finding anyone else like her for the rest of my life, and the pain and tenderness and heartache intensified. But I sat with that pain. For seven minutes. For ten minutes. For fifteen minutes. For eighteen long minutes. And afterward I felt some kind of relief. My tears dried. My cold sweat eased. My body stopped shaking, and a calmness set in. I fell asleep.

What happens when you keep facing your repressed fears, your sandbags, your dragons?

I have found that, in deepening my connection with my own repressed fears, I have been able to better question the meaning of my past. *Why did this have to happen to me? Why did I have that relationship? Why did I choose this career? Why did my parents treat me this way? Why did they allow that to happen to me? Why did they not care for me?*

When you dig deeper, you may also start to feel anger, rage, resentment, frustration, anxiety, sadness, grief, or shame. Questions might surface about how you were raised, or how you were mistreated, or how you weren't able to do what you wanted to do. You may wonder about missed opportunities. You might even relive the trauma of being abused, bullied, abandoned, manipulated, or dismissed. While you may have known how your past experiences affected your life at the mental and emotional level, you will now slowly start to realize and experience what the impact has been at the physical level. You might even conclude that some of your repressed fears were turned into chronic pain, constant tension, and illness in your body.

You are now getting the full picture of your past as reflected in the present: mentally, emotionally, and physically. Be mindful and observant of how your power starts to shift back to you as you slowly work through this process. You may still be inclined to hold your parents or other people responsible for your vulnerability and corresponding ailments or failures; such reactions are only natural. They are part of your journey. You are processing your past, digesting and integrating its pain and hurt. You are also shifting your energy and opening up your consciousness, preparing to rise from the subconscious to the self-conscious level. You may even be able to get glimpses of calmness, clarity, and balance on the horizon, but remember that, for now, your primary goal is to observe your physical sensations and sit with whatever may arise in your body.

DEALING WITH THE EMOTIONS
OF THE PAST

As part of your transition from subconscious to self-conscious, and as you work with the physical manifestations of your pain, a multitude of emotions will undoubtedly surface: anger, frustration, sadness, resentment, regret, guilt, or shame. This is especially common when we question our parents or other guardians, even if they did the best they could when raising us. And these childhood emotions, which have been locked down for so long, are often particularly intense and painful.

I'd like to guide you through dealing with them and appropriately discharging them from your body. Here's a list of suggested actions to help you expel them should they arise during your welcoming work.

Anger

What it is: Anger comes from the realization that, during your past painful, traumatic life experiences, others took your power away and made you feel powerless. You didn't know what to do or how to deal with them back then, so you gave in to their strength. Anger is a very forceful, primal, and physically charged emotion. It is so instinctive that it belongs to lower scales of consciousness, in the range of 15 to 20. In order to discharge such low-level emotions, you need to consciously use intense physical movements.

What you can do: Try air boxing, or punching a pillow, or consciously throwing tantrums by yourself in your room. Scream in the car, or shake your hands, arms, and legs as if you're trying to get rid of something. Jump up and down, or go for a sprint, or sweat heavily in the sauna. You can also explore other actions that get you in touch with your body and give you a sense of relief from charged-up energy.

Whatever you do, though, be very conscious. Conscious discharge means to stay connected with the anger and with the experience or the person that is the source of it while you're taking physical action to get rid of it. Sometimes you need to remember the situation and recall someone's face to re-charge the anger. In this way, you allow everything that has been repressed to surface again so you can fully discharge it. By NO means, and in NO event, should you direct your discharge at the situation or the person who hurt your feelings or caused you harm. In this charge-up process, the goal is not to throw blame on others for what they did to you, but rather to understand and connect with the force that past events caused within you, making you feel a certain way. Your conscious attention needs to be inward, to relate to that anger energy and to thoroughly discharge whatever is arising from your body. Practice detached self-observation to avoid getting too absorbed in the anger. You have used anger as an aggressive force to ward off triggers in the past and to attack people for what they did to you, but now, your attention must be turned inward to process that anger.

At the same time, remember, you are not the anger; you don't want to direct it at your Self or at others. Instead, try to tame that powerful force of anger, like a cowboy would tame a wild horse. Patiently, yet with strength and resilience, try to stay with the overwhelming discomfort that the emotional charge of anger creates, while consciously maintaining your connection to your body as you witness everything unfold as an objective observer.

Sadness

What it is: Sadness comes from the realization that you gave your power away to others to survive, to be safe, to belong. Sadness is created when you transact with others by giving your freedom or your power away in return for something necessary for your survival, as opposed to anger, which is created when others take your freedom or your power away and never give you anything in return. The painful experiences that created sadness actually made you feel like a victim who had to negotiate for survival. Your sadness has a soft, quiet energy. To process sadness, all you need to do is allow yourself to sob, cry, and shed tears until no tears are left to shed. Sadness invites you to quiet reflection, introspection, and contemplation. On the scale of consciousness, sadness often falls in the range of 25 to 30.

What you can do: To process sadness, sit down by yourself and write in your notebook whatever is arising. Maybe light a candle and play soft music while you reflect. Write down whatever surfaces about your sadness and let the tears flow naturally, whether gently or through uncontrollable sobbing. Keep consciously writing down whatever occurs to you until there is nothing more to add. Then try to go out for a walk and connect with nature. Find some trees in your neighborhood, or head out to a body of water: a pond, a river, a lake, or the ocean. Even as you notice the natural world, try to remain connected with the sadness in your body.

Guilt

What it is: Guilt naturally arises when you remember past experiences in which you hurt someone with your actions. Sometimes guilt may also surface about ways you've hurt yourself. In fact, it's not uncommon to feel guilty about betraying your subconscious and its comfort zone while learning to practice the techniques we've been discussing here. The exposure to guilt often comes later in your journey, in the 35 to 45 range.

Do not panic! You are still in transition. When you take new actions against your triggers, you may feel guilty, uneasy, and unsure of how things will flow from there. Now that you're taking your power back, what if you don't please others as much anymore? What if you stop trying to meet others' expectations all the time? What if you are no longer a perfectionist, and have gotten a little messy and careless? What if you don't drink as much as your friends? What if you don't watch TV as much as your significant other? What if you don't jump on every project offered at your job? As you respond to life from a different perspective, watch for the guilt that may surface as you challenge your Self and face the dragon.

What you can do: To discharge guilt, use the POWER Method as we've discussed so far. Sit with the discomfort that guilt creates in the body for as long as you can. Notice that you can do this longer as you slowly rise up on the scale of consciousness. As you sit with the physical sensations of the guilt, try to observe everything from a distance like a detached witness. Soon you will start to enjoy the glimpses of lightness resulting from the new alignment between your mind, heart, and body. When you're done, get up and shake your body, your arms, your hands, and your legs for a minute to discharge the guilt.

Shame

What it is: On the other side of guilt lies shame, waiting for you to come back to judge your Self for wrongdoing or foolish behavior that caused your pain and hurt in the past. This judgment is a natural defense mechanism your subconscious internal programming deploys so that you'll retreat into your comfort zone to avoid similar experiences in the future.

Shame is a fiery, toxic emotion that can burn you up and bring you down, even lower than anger. On the consciousness scale, shame ranges from 12 to 22. My invitation for you is to practice self-observation until you get hold of this powerful emotion. Try to establish your distance, that space we talked about, so you can gently observe your self-judgments and corresponding self-deprecating thoughts. Watch how low your self-worth goes.

Shame will make you beat your Self up so much that you become very stagnant.

What you can do: Get out of your head. Drop into your body. Where do you feel that stagnancy? Where do you feel shame in your body? To overcome this physical heaviness, you must tap into your body, literally. Stand up and tap the left side of your body with your right palm, starting with your upper body, then your arms, and then your head and face. Next switch to your left palm and tap the right side of your body. Finally, tap the back of your legs, the top of your feet, and along the inside of your legs. To end this tapping practice, jump up and down to shake off the energy, and to shake the shame out of your body.

One last quick note about welcoming your physical discomfort and facing your repressed fears: Don't be surprised if you start to shake. This phenomenon, a physical quaking like that of an aircraft trying to break the sound barrier, is quite common. It's a subtle movement of energy that causes this as your tissues, organs, and entire body try to digest all those repressed fears, along with other emotions, feelings, and memories buried deep within. Your body is being asked to face what it's most afraid of, what it's been running away from for so long. Be gentle with your body. Ride along from a detached but curious perspective, and simply let your body process as much as it can. When the shaking stops, which is usually after a few minutes, you may feel tired and thirsty. This means your body wants to rest. Take it easy and slow down. Drink a few cups of water. Make some nourishing, calming herbal tea. Take a nice hot shower. Soak in a bathtub. Listen to soothing music.

You are well on your way to cleansing all the sandbags, heaviness, and suffering that have been holding you back from a higher life for years. You are getting ready to embrace a New Life, a new future of your highest potential, one where you can connect with love, joy, fulfillment, meaning, and purpose. Ultimate Happiness is awaiting your arrival.

CHAPTER FIVE

EARTHING TO INTEGRATE YOUR POLARITIES

Imagine a society of human beings held captive in underground, cavelike dwellings, their necks and legs shackled so tightly they weren't even able to turn their heads. In Plato's "The Allegory of the Cave," a fire provides the only light for these prisoners, some of whom shuffle along a raised walkway, day and night. A wall along the far side of the path serves as a screen upon which their shadows are projected from the fire's light.

Now take a closer look at those people on the walkway: they are carrying a variety of artifacts made of stone, wood, and other materials, and they are talking as they walk. But the remaining people below the walkway can't see the walkers or what they're carrying, nor can the viewers hear what the walkers are saying. They can see only the shadows cast onto the wall and hear the voices echoing off it. The prisoners at ground level naturally believe the shadows they see are living, breathing creatures and the source of the sounds they hear. They have no reason to believe otherwise, to believe that the shadows aren't reflections of reality and the truth of life.

Since these prisoners have all been confined in the cave since childhood and have had nothing else to do but look at the shadows projected on the wall every day, they eventually invent a game to pass time. Honor, praise, and prizes are awarded to the prisoner who is best at identifying the shadows as they pass and predicting which shadow or object will come next. The winning prisoner is also granted power until the next time the game is played. But what if, one day, a prisoner gets fed up and bored with the game and the whole cave scene? What if they find a way to free themself from their shackles, stand up, turn their head, and identify a source of light near the cave's mouth? What if, as they head toward that light, it grows brighter? And what if they turn back to look into the cave and, because of the blinding light of the sun, they no longer see those shadows that they'd always thought were the truth? And what happens if the person steps outside the cave, adjusts their eyes, and starts to see a whole new world: land, lakes, animals, plants, sky? What if, under the clear light of day, they notice their own hands and feet? What if they look at their reflection in a nearby pond and see their face for the first time? Would these little steps of awakening to their own Real Self frighten them?

Could they slowly adapt to this new world? Could they accept the New Life as one comprising vivid colors, instead of sepia shadows? Would they realize their former view of reality was just an illusion—a puppet show completely made up by an unseen and unknown power to entertain the prisoners so they stayed in the cave for their lifetimes?

Imagine what might happen if the prisoner decided to go back to the cave, to inform the other prisoners of their findings. How do you think the others would react? In Plato's parable, the freed prisoner did return. And guess what? The remaining prisoners immediately dismissed them. They did not believe anything about this new reality that was allegedly found outside the cave. They cast the person out, even threatening to kill them if they tried to persuade them to go outside, away from their cave and games and routines, even if the motive was pure: to set them free.

What? Why would they cast the person away when all they were trying to do was invite them to freedom, to experience a more prosperous, abundant life in a vast new world?

The answer is simple: They were happy with the shadows and comfortable with the game they were playing. You see, the shadows are cast onto the wall so the prisoners don't *need* to know the real truth, the truth within themselves. The game entertains them, rewards them, gives them honor and praise for having the sharpest mind and the best memory. Even though the prisoners are confined in a dismal place, they enjoy living in the shadows and engaging in competitions because they are in their comfort zone.

I'm fascinated by how Plato's story so perfectly describes the life inside our subconscious realms: shadows dominate perception, projections become perceived realities, and limiting life patterns serve as fundamental elements of life in the cave. Like the cave, our subconscious consigns us to suffering and darkness and holds us back from our individual freedom, our highest potential, our Ultimate Happiness. And like the prisoners, maybe we aren't ready to leave our comfort zones. No one can drag us out if we're not ready.

This story also reminds me of the hero's journey. Imagine leaving your village, slaying the dragon, and discovering the high life beyond the forest. Then you return to your village and report what you found: a life filled with more light, more happiness, more joy, more fulfillment, and more meaning. What would the villagers do—your partner, your family, your parents, your friends, your boss, your colleagues, your neigh-bors, your community—when you invite them to venture into the new world with you? Would they believe you? Would they come with you? Would they leave their comfort zone? Or would they ignore your invitation and stay behind? What might frighten or threaten them about embarking on a journey of self-discovery and exploring higher levels of consciousness with you? What is the difficulty they'd need to overcome so they could take the first step?

Here's the thing: Everyone *seems* content and happy in the village with things as they are. Everyone *seems* to play their respective roles, conforming with the village's rules, wearing their respective masks, pretending to be someone or some-thing. Why would they want to leave? What they fail to rec-ognize, though, is that they're really hiding behind masks. Behind these masks, and within the confines of their well-defined roles, they believe they're safer in the village than in the lands beyond it, where they would face uncertainty and the unknown.

But as you have seen through your work so far, perceived reality doesn't reflect the true potential of a better life, which is only available at higher levels of consciousness. Fortunately, the System of Life doesn't leave anybody alone in their comfort zone. This system has been designed so that you *can* achieve self-actualization, attain self-realization. The way it runs, the way it flows into your life, sets you up to explore what's beyond your confining village walls. The problem is that some of us, in our subconscious minds, think we know better. We think we know how to protect ourselves against uncertainties. The System of Life doesn't give up on us; it continually offers us the gift of higher consciousness and Ultimate Happiness. Even so, most of us don't cash in that gift card and, instead, we allow our lives to be driven by repressed fears that con-fine us within the tight walls of our comfort zones. And sadly, most of us choose to remain there and keep running on the hamster wheel of limiting life patterns—even as they nudge us toward growth. And we rely on the masks we wear to hide our vulnerability, tricking ourselves into believing in our own self-created image, all the while feeling stuck, contracted, confused, and lost.

MASKS AS A SURVIVAL MECHANISM

What kind of masks have you been wearing to survive?

Masks are interesting concepts. When you look out through one, you often can't tell that you're wearing one. Only when you see your reflection in a mirror do you realize what you're hiding behind.

I remember when I was in the beginning of my transformation journey, one similar to the one that you're on today. I observed my Self out there, acting out my subconscious internal programming, and as I looked more closely at this Self, I saw someone, me, constantly anticipating others' behaviors. Shockingly, I noticed that I catered to others' needs and expectations all the time. I hadn't been aware of my mask, yet I not only complied with subtle signals of what I should be doing for these others, but I also went beyond their expectations. No wonder I felt so exhausted and depleted at the end of every day, even after some social family gatherings. I discovered I'd been doing things to impress and awe other people, craving approval, acceptance, inclusion, and intimacy.

In order to get to know my Self and discover my mask so I could understand who I was, I kept observing my Self from a distance in social situations, wondering why I was doing things the way I did. I eventually realized that I was a people pleaser. That was one of my masks: a person who wanted to make others happy no matter the personal cost. And I have to

say that I got what I wanted: I garnered the praise and com-
pliments I'd been looking for. I'd feel good about myself for
a second, but only for a quick second, because I'm also a shy
person. I wanted the positive feedback but would at the same
time cringe, not knowing what to do with the compliment. I'd
then return to my people-pleasing tendencies, which included
a close reading of faces and postures, and close listening to
tones of voice, to discern and anticipate what others might
want or need from me.

Masks are one of our survival mechanisms, along with
defensive actions and coping strategies. They serve as crutches
in our comfort zone, but they don't guide us along a path to
happiness. Wearing them simply makes us feel as though our
vulnerability is hidden, but in the end they result in conflict
and confusion, and they make us feel, once again, stuck within
our limiting life patterns.

Let's explore this a little bit more. As a people pleaser, my
goal has long been to impress others, to meet their expectations, to make them happy. To do this I have often decided—
whether consciously or not—to forego my own boundaries. I
have allowed the needs or desires of others to be more important than mine. I essentially gave part of my Self away to please
others, and that invariably led to a gathering resentment toward
them. Of course, I wouldn't often recognize this resentment
until they'd say something, or show a snarky attitude, or contradict me in some way, which would trigger me. I'd get mad,
sometimes even furious, and I'd take everything personally
and launch my defensive actions to lash out at them. Then I
would get into an argument with them, and the ensuing conflict would exhaust and deplete me. I'd also feel confused: how
could all of these efforts to please them yield so much turmoil?
All I'd wanted was connection, acceptance, and warmth, and
now we couldn't be further apart.

One of the most powerful limiting life patterns I've experienced started with my mom, a controlling figure. Deep down, I desperately wanted to make her happy by meeting her expectations. Her intentions were admirable; she wanted her son to be happy, and she tried to ensure this by imposing her values upon me. She thought she was guiding me to a better life. At the same time, I felt I had to relinquish my own values to satisfy hers, and for that matter, to satisfy my dad's, who you'll recall offered the *speak when you have something smart to say* guidance. I set out my entire life according to this subconscious internal programming: *If I give up my personal boundaries and values for others, I will get the connection, the acceptance, the recognition, the intimacy I desire.* So I wore the mask of a conforming, good, obedient son who did all the boring chores for the family, studied hard at school, didn't get into trouble, and followed his mom's every command, when sometimes I just wanted to chuck it all and run out to play with my friends. The mask, and giving up my boundaries, allowed me to stay in my comfort zone, but it also led to a lifetime of triggers and the resultant emotional reactions, a lifetime stranded in the cycle of pleasing others at the expense of losing my Self, which made me feel stuck, lost, and confused behind my people-pleaser mask. It wasn't until much later that I was able to look in the mirror and recognize the mask for what it was.

Law of Life #16:
Life is made up of relationships, and each
relationship is a mirror of your Self.

This phenomenon is part of your life. When we wear our masks for any reason, we give away part of our Self. That's the Self we want to recover in this journey to be *real* again. It's OK if your parents never recognized you, never saw you for who you were, never praised you. It's OK if they left you when you were young, if they controlled you or put you down. They might have planted your repressed fears of not being recognized, valued, good enough, seen, or worthy, and that's OK as well. Even if your parents led you to your fear of failure, it no longer matters, because now you understand how you designed and wore your masks to survive the pain.

Until now, you haven't really seen your masks because you were looking out at life, warding off triggers, defending against outside threats. As you begin to look inward, you will see your masks and understand why they've become part of your life. The prisoners in Plato's cave didn't want to abandon the life they'd grown accustomed to because they felt naked, vulnerable, and were terrified about leaving. And it's OK that they felt that way. Likewise, we don't need to shun our survival mechanisms, call our egos bad, or feel ashamed about our masks. We just need to embrace who we are and build our paths from this new, deeper understanding. We need to accept all of our faults and shortcomings and move into a higher consciousness, which will then allow us to view our past experiences as gifts contributing to a future, higher life—a life we all deserve to live.

THE UNMASKING PROCESS

The personality, the influence, and the force that sequester your repressed fears and make you wear a mask to disguise your vulnerability are what I call the *conditioned self.* Everybody has a conditioned, mask-wearing self. It's what we do to take our part in the "game" of life. Shakespeare also shared his view on life and the masks we wear in act 2, scene 7 of *As You Like*

It. "All the world's a stage and all the men and women merely players. They have their exits and their entrances; and one man in his time plays many parts."

Now that you understand the concept of repressed fears and have begun to think about yours, how would you describe your conditioned self, the part of you that hides repressed fears, or vulnerability, behind a mask? In order to answer this question, you need to go back to the question we were discussing earlier: Why do you do things the way you do? This *why* question opens the doors for you to meet your conditioned self face-to-face.

This new search can be considered an outward investigation, rather than an internal one. An internal investigation involves observing your emotions and thoughts, moving deeper into your repressed fears. In the outward investigation, you look in the opposite direction, observing the actions of your conditioned self in life, outside of yourself, to understand the *whys* behind your actions in order to reveal your mask.

You may be wondering where the conditioned self fits into the limiting life pattern cycle. It doesn't. The conditioned self is there all the time, whether or not we're triggered by any particular person or event. It guides how we live when we're living at the subconscious level. In my earlier story, for example, I was a people pleaser and my conditioned self always catered to other people's needs. But when they didn't appreciate what I'd done for them I got triggered, and the limiting life pattern was set into motion.

IDENTIFYING YOUR CONDITIONED SELF

How do you conduct an outward investigation to identify your conditioned self?

By asking *why* instead of *what if.* This style of question-ing is different from the previous internal investigation and provides you a slightly different perspective. You also don't have to wait until you're triggered to launch it. You don't even need to feel emotionally charged. All you need to do is observe yourself—and notice your mask—while doing something that leads you to a trigger. You just have to ask: *Why am I doing things the way I do?*

Your conditioned self is a little more difficult to spot than your repressed fears. Let me give you some examples of where you might find that self in some specific hypothetical situa-tions. But first, let me caution you that some of these scenarios may trigger defensiveness. If they do, use the first three steps of the POWER Method: PAUSE, OBSERVE, and WELCOME. Also, try to think about the *why* question, such as *why* someone would be a perfectionist, rather than wondering what's wrong with being a perfectionist. Be an objective observer; don't try to adjust or correct the conditioned self. Again, there's no right or wrong, good or bad. We all have a conditioned self that just wants to protect us from our vulnerability.

The invitation is to truly understand the conditioned self, and the masks you wear, so you can learn about your repressed fears. As you start to more deeply relate to your Self, you will begin to better understand the *why* and decode your subcon-scious internal programming even further.

Let's explore together some possible identities of the con-ditioned self.

Perfectionist

You're a *perfectionist.* You avoid any possibility of being seen as defective, disorganized, bad, or lacking integrity or discipline. You always want to excel at whatever you do. Instead of enjoying simple things, you turn everything you do into a task. For example, when you go on a nature hike, it's not about savoring the presence of mighty trees, wild animals, or the vast blue sky. It's about how fast you're going to complete the hike, how many calories you burn, how challenging the climb is. In other words, it's all about how good you are. You're obsessed with details: if pictures are hung on the wall properly, how well the wineglasses are sorted according to red, white, and rosé in your kitchen cabinet, or whether your spice jars are correctly stacked in alphabetical order in the drawer.

Repressed Fears: You have repressed fears of not having worth or not being good enough, appreciated, or recognized.

High Achiever

You are a *high achiever.* You dream big. You are ambitious. In whatever you do, you aim for the stars. You can accomplish so many things. You have so much firepower to get things done. You are imaginative and creative. You always have grand plans and strategies to accomplish things with energy and fire. For example, another lazy Sunday morning, and your partner just wants to sleep in a little bit, read the paper over a leisurely cup of coffee, and spend the rest of the day binge-watching TV. You, on the other hand, set your alarm to go off early so you can get the yard work done, pay the bills, and still have time for a ten-mile bike ride before dinner.

Repressed Fears: You have repressed fears of not accomplishing much in life, being an imposter, or being undeserving or unrecognized.

Approval Seeker

You are an *approval seeker.* You constantly look to your partner, your parents, or your friends for input or advice. You require a lot of encouragement to move forward with a project or venture. You feel uncomfortable if you do something outside of their expectations or their values. You feel paralyzed if there's no feedback loop for your actions or decisions. You're very indecisive, so that you might be afraid to paint your house a different color unless everyone you know agrees with your color choice.

Repressed Fears: You have repressed fears of not having worth or being a loser or a failure.

Controlling

You are a *controlling* person. You have high standards and see flaws in everything and everyone. You keep pointing out to others what they should or shouldn't do. "You shouldn't wear that!" or "You shouldn't have loaded the dishwasher that way." You are a critic, judging what's bad, what's wrong, what needs to be fixed all the time. You may even give unsolicited advice about how others should spend their time or what they need to do to better themselves. You also don't trust anyone to do things right; worse yet, you worry you'll be taken advantage of. You may closely observe your partner, criticizing their friends or how they spend money. When people don't meet your expectations, you are moody, judgmental, accusatory, and intimidating, often creating some sort of drama.

Repressed Fears: You have repressed fears of betrayal, being out of control, losing everything, failing, or being forced to live in a state of chaos.

People Pleaser

You are a *people pleaser.* You are constantly in service to people, accommodating them and placing their needs above everything else. You feel responsible for making people happy, and you burden yourself with a lot of tasks. You're uncomfortable when others are unhappy, and you often find yourself apologizing for their discomfort. You can't say no when others ask you to do something, even though you have tons of other stuff to do. You constantly feel what others need to such a degree that you may end up suffering financially when you loan out money to friends or family members, knowing that they'll never repay. You may always choose to be the designated driver when you go out with friends, sacrificing your happiness for others'.

Repressed Fears: You have repressed fears of loneliness, rejection, or dismissal; not being accepted or included; or not being good enough or liked.

Caregiver

You are a *caregiver*. You constantly feel that you
need to help others feel better, be better. You need
to fix what's broken, and you can't stand it when
someone is in discomfort or complains. You feel
called to step in with remedies to their problems.
Because you tend to see unhappiness all around
you, you might even go out of your way to take on a
martyr or savior role. You genuinely want others to
be happy, but you exhaust yourself with their bur-
dens as you ruminate about how to resolve their
issues. You may be one of the siblings who took care
of an ill parent, who didn't go to school because of
the duties you assumed at home: running errands
for them, taking them to doctor appointments,
and so on. In another situation, you may be a parent who ignores their own life for their grown-up
kids, coming to their rescue whenever the adult
child breaks up with a partner or loses a job.

Repressed Fears: You have repressed fears of loneliness, unhappiness, conflict, abandonment, or
being a disappointment to others. Your fears also
involve not having self-worth or being valued,
accepted, or adequate.

Procrastinator

You are a *procrastinator*. Your attention is everywhere and nowhere. You can't focus on the task at
hand. In other situations, your lack of focus, ded-
ication, and commitment makes you sluggish and
prevents you from attending to things until the

last minute, and then with a big rush of anxiety, insight, panic, and vision, you cram to complete your work just in time. You're prone to feeling lazy as you put things off as well as pressured to get things done. You're a master at finding excuses for not finishing the work: your car wouldn't start, the printer ran out of ink, and so on. You also tend to spend time engaging in unproductive activities like watching TV, lounging leisurely, calling friends to hang out, or doing anything else to avoid focusing on your project.

Repressed Fears: You have repressed fears of both failure and success, of not being recognized or having self-worth, and of missing out on life.

Social Butterfly

You are a *social butterfly.* You are friendly, personable, charming, persuasive, talkative, and optimistic. You are a big networker. You know everyone. You have many friends in many places, and wherever you go, you're the life of the party. You like meeting and staying in touch with a lot of people. You like organizing events to bring people together, and you have no problem striking up conversations with strangers. You may be impulsive and spontaneous, changing your mind often and going wherever the wind carries you, and people might think of you as irresponsible, making it hard for them to trust you. On the other hand, you are an interesting person with many hobbies, and always on your way to a new adventure. Among your friends or your colleagues at work, you may be the only one who belongs to a tennis club, who has a yacht docked in the downtown marina, or who belongs to the most exclusive social club in town.

Repressed Fears: You have repressed fears of loneliness, betrayal, rejection, abandonment, or missing out on life. You may also be afraid of being an imposter.

Know-It-All

You *know it all.* Period. You tell everyone how to live. You opine on things and give advice to others, and you dismiss others' opinions, suggestions, and comments. You live in a black-and-white world, where you judge things as good or bad, smart or stupid. Your belief and value system is objective and absolute; therefore, you think you are always right, especially because you read a lot to stay informed, you learn quickly, and you have a sharp, strong memory. But you are also competitive, thinking you do everything better than anyone else. You talk too much, giving little time for others to chime in, and when they do, you don't listen because you don't find people interesting. You may be a bookworm or intellectual with a certain seriousness about politics and life sciences, either putting others down for their lack of knowledge or dismissing them for their ignorance. Due to your highly intellectualized image of your Self, you may feel lonely and stranded at times.

Repressed Fears: You have repressed fears of not being recognized, important, understood, or accepted. You are also afraid of being a failure or being marginalized or excluded.

Always Late

You are *always late*. You've got lots going on at any given time. You want to be everywhere at once, and you tend to underestimate how long tasks will take. You take on too many different projects. You strive to be a multitasker, but without success when it comes to time management, so you're always in a rush. Quite often, you may decide to send just one more email before you leave the office at night, or take one more sip of coffee before you leave home in the morning, or read one more interesting article before meeting up with a friend, and then it's rush, rush, rush—and invariably you're late.

Repressed Fears: You have repressed fears of missing out on things, being a failure, not getting things done, not being recognized, or not being seen.

Aloof

You are *aloof.* You are someone who withdraws from people or has a hard time connecting with them. You establish just a few deep relationships with friends or family members. You are cautious getting into new relationships, needing to slowly build trust over time. You have a sixth sense for assessing situations and people that are potentially hurtful. You're also always on the outside of the clique, and you put up walls to protect yourself from getting hurt. You might even think everyone is out to get you. Therefore, you live most of your life hiding from others, rarely leaving your home, declining party invitations, doing most of your shopping online, and not returning any of your friends' phone calls.

Repressed Fears: You have repressed fears of abandonment, betrayal, rejection, being misunderstood, being an imposter, not having self-worth, or not being important.

The roles that the conditioned self assumes, like the ones described above, are reflected in the masks we wear. And of course there are many more. Others you might find familiar include the penny pincher, conflict avoider, narcissist, or worrier, or people who are described as happy-go-lucky, judgmental, bored easily, messy, or addictive.

So who is *your* conditioned self? Which ones do you relate to? I invite you to keep digging deeper, to keep observing your actions and reactions. You might also look around and ask yourself if you know anyone in your family or circle of friends who wears some of these masks.

Life Skills Assignment #9:
Get to know your conditioned self and
understand why you act the way you do.

In your daily review, write down the conditioned self you observed during the day. First, call out its name and describe the way it shows up in your life. Then identify the repressed fears that your conditioned self tries to hide. And finally, reflect on your early memories to discover the origins of the fears that you've been carrying your entire life. For example:

Name of the conditioned self: Controlling

The way you act: I notice my controlling tendencies when I feel uneasy and things don't go the way I want them to. I immediately jump into the situation and start telling everyone what to do, or I judge them for not doing the things I want them to do. Sometimes I end up doing everything by myself because no one else can do as good of a job as me.

Repressed fears: I realized that I have repressed fears of being betrayed, being in chaos, being out of control, being exposed to unexpected circumstances or uncertainty.

Origins: The tendency to control things might have stemmed from my childhood. I was around nine years old when my dad told me not to trust anyone and that I should do things my own way. He had all the reasons not to trust others. I remember he had a bad fallout with one of his business partners. They broke off their partnership after my dad found out that his partner had been withdrawing money from the business account for his personal affairs. Since then, I've always thought people could take advantage of me or betray me and therefore I tend to feel unsafe when I don't have control.

THE FORCE BEHIND THE CONDITIONED SELF

Let's say you're a high achiever. That means you're running away from the fears of being an imposter, or of not being deserving or recognized, or of not having accomplished anything in life. So you've created this mask, a high-achieving conditioned self, to hide your vulnerability. But you can't just passively wear a mask and go about your day. The mask requires a force behind it to get you to take action.

What kind of force do you think will offset the fear of being an imposter, for example? You would want to accomplish things to prove that you're not an imposter. You might be competitive in order to show that you're better than others. You'd probably always be rolling up your sleeves to get things done, be recognized, and rise to the top. The force behind all these actions is what I call *hidden desires*.

Hidden desires are the force that creates the conditioned self. As a result, they're part of your survival mechanisms. There's nothing wrong with having hidden desires, but you will never be able to fulfill them because they are part of your subconscious internal programming and not a product of your higher consciousness. You keep feeding your hidden desires with certain actions and attachments as you work to cover up your vulnerability, and therefore you're always on the defense, on the run to avoid getting hurt. This makes your life fearful instead of fulfilling.

For example, if you have a fear of not being recognized, you may end up wearing the mask of a high achiever as the force behind your hidden desires. At the same time, you will always subconsciously be on the lookout for people or situations that will challenge your accomplishments. You will have to face them over and over as part of your limiting life patterns, as yet another invitation to figure out your repressed fears. Your hidden desires become reinforced each time you face those people or situations, and until you understand the connection between repressed fears and hidden desires, you'll continue to swing back and forth between them, feeling stuck and confused because you're certain you've been doing everything possible to achieve higher accomplishments, but you never quite get there.

I was a night owl for much of my life. I would stay up until after midnight, watching TV, surfing the internet, doing some work, reading about the Golden State Warriors, or trading players for my fantasy football team. Then I would get up early in the morning to beat the rush-hour traffic from my home in San Francisco to my job in Palo Alto. Tired, exhausted, and depleted from lack of sleep and from looking at the computer screen all night long, I would be agitated and anxious throughout the entire one-hour commute.

When I started doing my transformation work on my conditioned self, I questioned why I was a night owl. I used to tell everyone that I've never been a morning person. That was my excuse. But why? So I kept observing what I was getting from staying up so late. Eventually I realized my hidden desire. There I was, in the corporate world, doing accounting and finance work. I wasn't fulfilled. Something was missing. I was feeling the void. I was missing fun, fulfillment, and meaning. Since I wasn't finding these hidden desires at work, I had begun looking for them in the wee hours of the night, but I wasn't aware this was what I was doing. Instead of figuring out why I was a night owl, I kept wearing the night-owl mask of my conditioned self to avoid facing my vulnerability and the truth that I didn't like my career. It was scary because I didn't know what else to do, and I completely depended on my career because of my fear of financial instability. I'm happy to share with you now that I'm no longer a night owl; in fact, I'm an avid morning person. I love the freshness and calmness of the mornings.

Another one of my conditioned selves was "always being late." No matter what I did, I would always run two or three minutes late to all meetings and appointments. It didn't matter whether it was a business meeting or a personal meeting with a friend. Again, asking the question why, I realized that I didn't own my time. Whenever I was about to leave one place and head for another, I'd remember the urgent email I'd forgotten to send or one more chore that needed to be done. Something always needed to be handled before I could get on with my plans. Of course, I was frustrated that I didn't have the discipline to put myself in a better position. At last, I realized that it was my conditioned self—whose hidden desire was to get a lot of things done within the limited time available. As soon as I made this connection, I was better able to prioritize my work. I began managing my time so that I didn't have to rush anymore. I started to get into the flow. Granted, no one is perfect, and I still occasionally run late to meetings, but now I can recognize the force that distracts me and understand the hidden desires behind my lateness.

Life can definitely seem paradoxical. You try to hide your vulnerability; you wear a variety of masks. And what does life do? It brings people or situations into your experience that poke at your vulnerability—the very thing you're trying to hide.

What is the message of life here?

Law of Life #17:
Life is full of opportunities for deeper
understanding of why we do things the way we do.

Let's dig deeper into this message, courtesy of life.

For a long time, I used to be controlling in my relationships. I had the attitude of *my way or the highway*, trying to ensure everything would be in order, and everyone would be doing what they were supposed to do. It was ironically fitting that, for a while, my official corporate job title was corporate controller, even though what I was doing was not fulfilling for me.

Life was nudging me to examine my controlling tendencies, but I didn't have a clue how to read her messages or hear her guidance. Also, I didn't have the capacity or the option to behave another way. My controlling conditioned self had some pretty high standards and ideals about how people should behave and how things should flow. As a result, my focus would be directed outward at others—what they were doing, whether I could trust them, and how I should tell them what to do.

This tendency to be judgmental about other people, including my partner, in turn generated a lot of anxiety in my relationships. Even though my hidden desire was to make everything smooth for both of us, and to provide comfort and stability for the relationship, I found myself continually criticizing her and asking, "Why did you do this?" or "Why did you do that?" This force—my hidden desire—got pretty annoying to her after a while, as I was most likely triggering her repressed fears of being controlled with my controlling conditioned self.

Even though my partner would be annoyed, she'd often gently ask me to back off a little bit and assure me that everything was "under control." But instead of lessening my fears, her response would trigger me even more. I'd take it personally, thinking that she was accusing me of being a bad, controlling partner. Her criticism would make me feel unappreciated. I'd get angry and defend myself by either blaming her for minor things or leaving the room to avoid an argument. The conflict would continue for a few hours and would leave me confused about my relationship, what I was doing wrong, or whether she was the right partner for me. All of this happened in my own perceived reality. In fact, it was my own controlling conditioned self that initiated the trigger event by provoking her repressed fears and emotional reactions. The message? I needed to learn about my own controlling tendencies, and my underlying repressed fears and hidden desires.

Similar relationship patterns plague millions of couples. Unintentionally and unconsciously, we trigger each other while we're trying to execute our own survival mechanisms, in the form of defensive actions, coping strategies, and the conditioned self. After every argument, conflict, and limiting life pattern cycle, we feel confused about our relationship and our partner, and we question if they are the right one for us. Yet we ignore the underlying currents of subconscious internal programming and the inner workings of our conditioned self. The masks we wear hamper our ability to see the truth; instead, we get lost in our perceived realities and miss out on the opportunity to really get to know our Self, as well as each other.

The bottom line is that we each unconsciously create our own conflicts because our conditioned selves are designed to behave defensively. Their motives are to survive, and they use our hidden desires to propel the hot air balloon higher, away from suffering, for temporary relief while we assume the roles of perfectionist, people pleaser, and so on. But after a while, because we haven't released our sandbags, one thing or another will happen to trigger us, and our sandbags will pull us down to lower altitudes yet again.

RESOLVING YOUR INTERNAL CONFLICTS

As we reviewed earlier, internal conflict is the primary source of your limiting life patterns. As shown in the previous examples, you do your best to hide your vulnerability by wearing your conditioned self's mask. Yet people always seem to find your tender spot and provoke your repressed fears. You blame them for triggering you and slip into your perceived reality and limiting life pattern cycle. By the time you've reached the end of the cycle, you wonder what else you can do to avoid these people and their attitudes, harsh tones, judgmental comments, and critical observations. I've often heard others say, when they complain about their significant others, "I don't know how they know it, but what they do is exactly what pisses me off. And they still do it."

This internal conflict feels like a pendulum that swings from one polarity to another, pulling you between your repressed fears and your hidden desires. In other words, acting out your conditioned self—as a perfectionist, people pleaser, and so on—only serves to reinforce the limiting life patterns and corresponding defensive actions that are actually intended to ward off triggers that might lead to conflict.

And the examples of this internal conflict are plenty in life:

You have a fear of not being good enough. Your hidden desire is to work hard to be perfect. But you keep attracting people who criticize you and disregard your hard work.

You have a fear of loneliness. Your hidden desire is to be in a relationship so that you don't feel lonely. But you keep dating people who may not be willing to commit to a long-term relationship.

You have a fear of failure. Your hidden desire is to be successful. You earn certifications and diplomas, land great jobs, or start your own business, yet obstacles that feel like failure always appear: your

diplomas become obsolete, you get fired, or you go
bankrupt.

You have a fear of having low self-worth. Your hidden desire is to be appreciated, valued by someone. So you keep falling for people who treat you
well in the beginning but then turn into monsters
who mistreat you, demean you, and make you feel
less-than.

You have a fear of abandonment. Your hidden desire
is to hedge the risk of being abandoned. You surround yourself with many friends, yet because
they're not close, they end up betraying you,
dismissing you, or otherwise making you feel
abandoned.

When you take a step back and look at these examples, you
can't help but sense the possibility that this internal conflict,
though painful and restrictive in nature, can serve as a gate-
way, clue, or invitation to further explore the very suffering
you want to run away from.

Law of Life #18:
Suffering in life is a direct result of the
internal conflict between repressed
fears and hidden desires.

What can you do about this conflict?

You can learn to integrate your repressed fears and your
hidden desires.

Imagine a tall, strong tree in a mighty wind. It bends with the force of every gust, yet it comes back to its center. Why? It has strong roots that connect the body of the tree to the earth. The roots ground the tree while also nourishing it and ensuring its vitality.

Now, sitting or standing, place your feet flat on the floor. Feel the ground underneath your feet. Close your eyes and sense the earth holding your feet, supporting your body, and giving you a sense of centeredness. That's the feeling of being grounded. You can go back to this feeling any time by just directing your attention to the bottoms of your feet to connect with the earth. This works whether you're inside or outdoors; you don't have to literally be touching soil.

The integration of your polarities—your repressed fears and hidden desires—will come about through this grounding process. Gravity and the solidity of the earth hold these two opposing forces together. They also provide a sturdy base to stand on as you face your triggers from a state of tranquility, a state of strong presence, which allows you to let go of your sandbags; this base empowers you to resist getting hooked by triggers and, subsequently, pull out of the vicious cycle. As a result, you break free from your limiting life patterns and rise into higher consciousness, where you start to feel your own presence, and get a glimpse of Ultimate Happiness.

Law of Life #19:
Integration of polarities creates presence through a deeper alignment between mind, heart, and body.

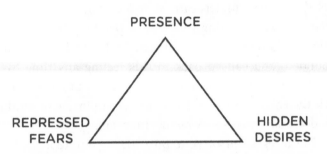

While this sounds sensible on the page, it's through your own experience that you can truly sense how powerful the earth can be in integrating your repressed fears and hidden desires. Let's practice.

> **Life Skills Assignment #10:**
> **Integrate the opposing forces of your repressed fears and hidden desires.**

Select a trigger event from your day. Start by tracing the emotional charge to your body, as we've practiced earlier, and then follow the instructions below (i.e., entry number 9 and after, to apply the integration process steps to your repressed fears and hidden desires). Write down your findings and how you felt after the integration process in your daily review journal.

Here's a real-life example from a procrastinator's notebook:

Today's Date: November 11, 2020
1. Emotion: Anxiety, anger, frustration.
2. Trigger: I don't seem to be motivated to work on my project today. I'm spending a lot of time doing other stuff instead of my project.
3. Thought: I don't see this project going anywhere. I think I'm not going to be successful at completing all its bits and pieces. I have already lost some credibility by not getting it done by now. The project is not as interesting as I thought it would be. I don't have the energy or the necessary self-worth to complete it.
4. Repressed Fear: Fear of failure, fear of success, fear of being judged or not having self-worth.
5. Origins: Growing up, I learned to get by with the least amount of study. After making a big push to be at the top of my class, and then failing, I gave up studying that hard. I lacked the self-discipline to allocate consistent time to my studies. Maybe I lacked competitive spirit because of my struggle with self-esteem and self-worth. Nonetheless, I figured out that twenty percent effort got me seventy percent there in terms of grades. My parents never encouraged me to study hard, so I drifted into more leisurely school routines, rather than focused ones that would have led to success and accomplishment.
6. Body Part: I felt my anxiety, anger, and frustration in my stomach.
7. Sensation: As I tuned into the emotional charge in my stomach, I discerned tension, heaviness, and contraction. Calmly observing the sensations, I could tell that it was getting up there in intensity. I'd say around 7 on a scale of 1 to 10.

Your next step will involve welcoming the emotional charge that the trigger has caused in your body. Then loosen its intensity by discharging some of it through a simple inhale and exhale. Here's what our procrastinator had for his entry number 8:

8. Welcome: I took a deep breath into the physical sensation in my stomach and held it for three seconds. At this moment, I was connecting with the heaviness I was feeling. Then I exhaled it from the back of my throat and out through my mouth with a lion's roar, at the same time pushing the charge out of my body through the bottoms of my feet into the earth. I repeated this routine two more times. This quick breath release loosened the intensity of my repressed fear. I now could access its energy. I was surprised that the intensity of my physical sensations dropped from 7 to 4 after this quick three-by-three breath work. I felt a little lighter. The sensation seemed to continue to be lessening as I observed the sensations in my body. I knew I wasn't completely releasing or expelling the emotional charge, but just cracking its shell to access and work with the repressed fears buried in my stomach.

After you do this three-by-three breath work to welcome the charge and loosen its intensity, you're ready to begin the integration process, which will become the ninth entry in your daily review journal. Because it's a process, let's take a break from reading our procrastinator's notebook and just walk through the steps of integration one by one:

9. Name the force of the repressed fear: Start by reconnecting with the physical sensations you felt earlier. Notice the intensity again and then transport it into your *right* palm. This transport process is a relocation of energy, as if you're relocating furniture from one house to another. Pull up the truck, load it, and move whatever remained after your breath work into the truck, or your right hand. Feel it. Sense the transfer. Once it seems you've captured the whole emotional charge in your right palm, contain it by making a fist.

Now label the energy you're holding in your fist. What would you like to call it? What name, word, or phrase would describe this energy, this sensation the best way? What kind of feelings does the trigger event provoke in you? Pay attention to the quality and nature of the energy you captured in your right palm. Words and phrases such as heaviness, darkness, trapped, isolation, hiding under the table, contracted, lonely, oppression, and little are some of the common ones that I've heard from my clients over the years. Choose your own words to describe how this energy feels to you. By naming it, you take ownership of it, and this in turn will help you integrate the polar opposite forces of repressed fears and hidden desires. Let's use the word *trapped* to label how procrastination makes us feel contracted and boxed in.

It's important to note that you want to keep the emotional charge's intensity as high as possible at this point because your goal will be to integrate your positive energy with your negative energy—in other words, your hidden desires and your repressed fears—and if you release too soon, there's nothing to integrate. This is true even if the opposing forces aren't equal in strength, which is often the case because your survival mechanisms, and corresponding repressed fears, have been operating since birth, whereas hidden desires often develop later. In my experience, the intensity of my repressed fears is usually about eight times stronger than the intensity of my hidden desires.

Once you've named the energy, to close the transfer of the energy related to your repressed fear to your right fist, softly inhale and exhale the remaining charge out of your body through the bottoms of your feet into the earth, making sure not much contraction or tension remains in the body part where you felt the emotional charge before. Keep your right fist relatively tight.

10. Name the opposing force of hidden desires: Next, connect with the opposite energy of what you're holding in your right fist. We named it *trapped* (see entry 9 above). What would be the opposite of that? Describe the opposite energy, using one word or phrase again. Let's call it *freedom*. There's no right or wrong answer here. You may choose other words or phrases that describe the way you feel, the way your hidden desires speak to you. Maybe *flow*, *success*, or *openness*, for example, will resonate with you more. Feel into it and choose one.

11. Body part, the place where hidden desires appear: Then locate that opposite energy in your body. Where was the sensation, the feeling of *freedom* in the body? Initially, you may not be able to easily find it. If so, try to recall when you last felt a sense of freedom. If you can't find a moment that brings up memories of freedom, then simply imagine or visualize a situation that could bring a sensation of freedom to you. Note that this is the most challenging task of the integration process because the strength of these forces is often quite lopsided. Like we discussed above, the force of a repressed

fear feels like an ocean, compared to the force of a hidden desire, which feels more like a lake. Can you remember a moment of freedom? Go back to that moment and imagine the physical sensation that feeling created in your body. Most probably, it will be in your heart, or all over your body. Just tune in to any physical sensation that you experience when you connect with a sense of freedom. Where is it in your body?

After locating the physical sensation of this positive force, transport it into your *left* palm by planting your feet, inhaling, and exhaling. Make a tight fist to thoroughly capture it and contain it. Check in with your body to see if the positive charge has cleared out of your body and into your hand. If not, repeat. Whereas the previous exercise, to transfer the negative energy of your repressed fears into your right palm, was to crack the shell that's been stored for years, this stage of the exercise is designed to neutralize your body and prepare it for integration.

By now you're ready for the final steps of the integration process, your fists still tightly closed.

12. Alternate focus between fists/opposing forces: These last steps are all about your ability to focus. Your self-observation meditation work will pay huge dividends here. With both hands in fists, first focus on your right palm, connecting with the energy that you're holding there. Sense the feeling, *trapped*, that you've identified before, and try to feel it with your body for three seconds. Then shift your focus to your left palm and focus on the energy, the feeling of *freedom* that you've connected to earlier, for another three seconds. Alternate your focus back and forth between your

right and left palms three times, sensing the energy in your fists on every focus.

13. Integration through the earth: Once you're done with the three cycles, which I call three-by-three focus work, pause for a few seconds. Bring your focus to the bottoms of your feet. Ground yourself. Get ready to do three-by-three breath work, while holding both of your fists tight. Take a deep breath in, imagining fresh air and new energy flowing into your body, from your feet all the way up to your crown. Then hold your breath for three seconds while focusing on your crown and feeling the energies of *being trapped* and *being free* at the same time. Tighten your fists slightly, so you can sense these energies even more intimately. Then exhale and bring your focus back to the bottoms of your feet. Connect with the earth. Keep your fists tight.

Before you complete your three-by-three breath work, let me share with you a little trick for your integration step. While focusing on your crown, the trick is to be able to think about both palms at the same time. How can you do that? How can you hold your focus on the top of your head while also thinking about being trapped and being free? In order to successfully integrate these opposing forces, you want to hold both of them together in your mind. Only then will they melt together, and you will have neutralized these energies in your body. Maybe you can imagine putting one of your hands into a bucket of warm water and the other into a bucket of cold water. Can you now feel the different temperatures of each bucket of water, and sense the average temperature as if they had been poured into one bucket? While thinking about both of them, try to look at them with your inner gaze, which is similar to the inward attention you practice in self-observation meditation, keeping your eyes closed and connecting with the physical sensations.

I call this a "trick" because you may have never held your focus on two separate things at the same time. Focusing on both charges, both names, both opposites, both energies at the same time means holding them in your mind as a sensation, *not* as a thought. Try to use your body to sense both fists and both energies, instead of imagining them with your mind. Don't expect miracles on your first go! If you struggle, practice self-observation a little longer. Within a few days, you'll feel a subtle shift in your ability to hold your focus on both fists at the same time.

14. Release of sandbags to rise in consciousness: To finish the integration process, do the remaining two cycles of your three-by-three breath work. Each time, remember to hold your breath for three seconds while focusing on your crown and connecting with your fists, and then simply exhale. In the final cycle, when you're exhaling, release your fists and all the emotional charges you've been holding in your palms out through your feet and into the earth. Bring your focus to the bottoms of your feet and stay connected with the earth for a few seconds, or even a few minutes, until you feel centered and grounded. When you're ready, return to your daily review journal.

15. Describe your state of being, your presence: Write down your state of being after the integration process—how you feel mentally, emotionally, and physically, as well as any thoughts floating through your mind. After the integration process, you may feel a little dizzy and tired— due to your rise in consciousness. Your body

is trying to recover and heal from the release of
sandbags. Drink a lot of water and then lie down
for some time, maybe for fifteen to thirty minutes. Alternatively, you may feel lighter, as if the
heaviness of your repressed fears has left your
body. In that lightness, your heart and your mind
are being integrated. If you were procrastinating,
let's say, you may find extra energy to go back to
your project and start working on it. You may
have no thoughts of whether you're going to fail or
succeed—you will simply connect with your project at a deeper level and want to make some progress on it.

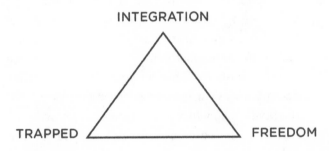

The integration process is an important part of your journey through consciousness. Therefore, let's spend some time
discussing some common questions about this process.

*What is the relationship between the first and second emo-
tional charge?*
Let's assume that you had the same conditioned self, the
procrastinator. Your first physical sensation, which we named
trapped, came from your emotional reaction to procrastination and your repressed fear of being a failure. It showed up as
a contraction in your stomach. Your second emotional charge,
which we named *freedom*, reflected your hidden desires, or

the opposite of your repressed fears. That's why you name the energy of the repressed fears first, then find the opposite of that name or phrase to identify your hidden fears. In this case, your hidden desires would be *wanting to be a success*, believing that success would liberate you from your repressed fears, and you would feel *freedom*. This hidden desire for success manifested in your chest as a physical sensation. And don't be surprised if both of your emotional charges, even though they are the opposite of each other, appear in the same spot in your body. After all, they are different sides of the same coin, products of the same subconscious internal programming.

Does the integration process take place anywhere outside the body?

No. It happens in the body, nowhere else. Not in the mind. Not in the heart. As a matter of fact, with this process, you bring your lower subconscious mind—where your repressed fears live—and your subconscious heart—where your hidden desires lie—together. Integration means aligning them with each other so that you can release your sandbags and rise above subconscious to self-conscious. In a sense, your repressed fears and hidden desires are in the mind and heart of your subconscious, respectively, yet manifest together physically in your body.

Why do you want to integrate these opposing forces as sensations within your body, and not as thoughts in your mind?

Because you feel the forces that your repressed fears and hidden desires create within your body; in other words, that's where they've been stored, that's where they manifest, and that's where they take your power away. When these two opposing forces created by your subconscious survival mechanisms pull your body into two different directions, you get off-center. You give in to your defensive fight-or-flight responses. As a result, you deplete your energy. Your body feels weak and becomes obedient to the orders of your subconscious. That's why you sometimes lose control over your actions and do things you regret afterward.

All of that conflict is happening within the body. One force is fear-based and pulls you back, like in our example above: the fear of being a failure making you feel *trapped* and pulling you back into a procrastination state. Then, you become mentally paralyzed by this fear-based force, and physically feel heavy and lazy and can't pull yourself up to work on your project.

On the other hand, the opposing force is desire-based and pushes you forward. In this case, the hidden desire is to be successful. You may connect with this force as a feeling of expansion. That's why you felt a sense of *freedom*. You want to advance in your project. Deep down, you're attached to its success, because it would prove that you're not a failure. Repressed fears create a victim state. Hidden desires create a state of attachment. Both manifest in the body.

Throughout your life, you have been controlled by these opposing forces, both of which are subconscious fight-or-flight responses. You have swung between these two polarities, leaving you stuck, lost, and confused in your mind but also conflicted and suffering in your body. That's why it is very important to integrate the opposing forces of repressed fears and hidden desires as sensations within your body, and not as thoughts. Through integration, you reverse engineer the whole flow from the subconscious mind to the body, so that you neutralize the effects of your subconscious internal programming, and your survival mechanisms no longer control your actions. You take power back into your hands, hence the name POWER Method. You make your own decisions about how to live within the world based on your developing self-awareness and deeper understanding of Self as your level of consciousness rises.

Law of Life #20:
Rising toward higher consciousness naturally takes place through the integration of opposing forces, where you find presence.

Why is life on our side? How does life lead us toward Ultimate Happiness?

We've been exploring these questions in detail and from different perspectives. Now, I believe, in order to truly answer these questions, it would be beneficial for you to observe a few real-life sessions where you can witness the results that one of my clients experienced after a thorough integration process.

FRIDA'S STORY

It was Tuesday, a rainy fall morning, when Frida walked into my office with red, puffy eyes. She had been struggling with painful grief over her father's passing due to a sudden, unfortunate accident a few years earlier. Sunday marked the three-year anniversary of his death. I could tell she was still wearing the heaviness of not having him in her life.

In our first meeting, Frida asked me how to handle the grief that was so strong even after three years. I asked her to go back in time and tell me the exact moment when she heard about her father's fatal accident. She remembered it immediately and was visibly triggered. I invited her to PAUSE to notice the emotions she felt in that moment, right then and there. An immense sadness came over her. She then OBSERVED the thoughts that were going through her mind when she heard the news. "What am I going to do now? I lost my anchor in life. I lost someone who truly sees me, recognizes me, motivates me, knows me. I lost someone I trust. I lost a deep connection with a great human being. I don't know life without my father."

I invited her to acknowledge that deep sorrow, that painful sadness these thoughts created in her. She was able to drop into her body and feel the contraction and heaviness in the center of her chest. I asked her the intensity of the pain that her sadness created. She labeled it a 9 on a scale of 1 to 10. I walked her through the three-by-three breath work and asked her to start by inhaling into the physical sensation. I encouraged her to WELCOME it into her body. And then I coached her to exhale it out of her feet into the floor, to ground the charge from her body into the EARTH.

She did her three-by-three breath work for three seconds at a time, for three repetitions, each time sitting with the sadness. Right after her third exhale, her face was no longer tense and her shoulders had relaxed quite a bit. When I inquired about the intensity of her pain this time, and the sadness it created, she said it was now at 3 or 4.

When I greeted Frida again for our second session, I noticed she looked extremely annoyed. I thought maybe we'd gone too far in the first session and opened up her repressed fears too much. But this wasn't the case. She loved our first session and actually had used the POWER technique a few more times during the week whenever she felt heavy sadness in her chest. She shared that the memories of her father hadn't triggered her grief as much. She had been able to think about her father more peacefully, and she'd felt more grounded throughout the week.

I wasn't surprised; this wasn't the first time a client responded so positively to an emotion that they'd been struggling with for a long time. But I was a little puzzled as to why she looked so annoyed. So I asked how she was feeling.

"I'm pissed right now," she said. "I always feel like people have an agenda against me. They always treat me with some demeaning attitude. I'm so annoyed with people. I feel like it's because I'm a young, female manager, different from all the men at the company, and on top of that, I'm not white."

I wrote down the emotion as *anger* and the trigger as *people's demeaning attitudes*. I then inquired about her thoughts.

"Whenever I deal with these people, and face these attitudes, I always feel disrespected, dismissed, not seen." I noted the *feeling of being disrespected* as her thoughts.

I asked where she felt her anger in her body. She said it was in her chest and throat.

"Where is it most intense?" I asked.

"In my throat. It's hard to swallow. It makes my mouth dry." She rated it a 7.5 on the intensity scale of 1 to 10, and she likened it in size to an apple. But instead of being a brilliant red or enticing green, its emotional charge was brown.

I asked her to return to an incident when she faced these demeaning attitudes, advising her to simply pay attention to herself and not to others.

"I'm hunched over, my head feels heavy. I feel pressure across my shoulders. I'm speechless, withdrawn, and uneasy. Scattered. And also trapped. I'm so angry that I can't get anything done, not even basic things."

Next, I invited her to acknowledge the heaviness and the blockage in her throat. While sitting with these sensations, I asked her if she had any memories from her past that made her feel similarly angry, annoyed, demeaned, dismissed, or not respected.

She almost screamed. "Yes! My mom always validated my brother growing up. She would praise him even if he took the trash out—and whatever I did passed unnoticed. My mom never recognized me. She never acknowledged my achievements. She never saw who I was."

After reconnecting with a memory that tied to her feelings today, I guided her through the POWER Method. I reminded her to follow the three-by-three breath work again, all the while keeping the bottoms of her feet connected to the earth. And then it was time for the integration process. I walked her through each step to identify the opposing forces that created her internal conflict and caused her to be out of balance and off-center.

We started the integration process at the throat, where she felt her anger that was provoked by the thought of being disrespected, one of her primary repressed fears.

"Now, using your imagination, transport all of the charge from your throat into your right hand, and then make a fist to capture the energy of disrespect," I suggested. Then I asked what she wanted to call that feeling in her right palm.

"Nobody."

She then named the opposing energy, representing her hidden desire.

"Everyone."

I guided her to make it a little bit more personal. "For example, if you are disrespected and not seen, that means you are nobody. What is the word that describes the opposite—the feeling of being respected, being seen?"

"Somebody."

She then went back into her past to identify a time when she had felt like somebody. It was when she'd been the president of her student council, and she now felt that physical, positive energy in her heart. This was what she transported to her left hand.

Now she was holding her repressed fear of being disrespected, being nobody, in her right fist and her hidden desire of being seen and being somebody in her left fist. She did her three-by-three focus work, alternating between each hand, placing her focus on each fist for three seconds, for three cycles. It was time for integration. Before we started, I asked her to ground herself by bringing her attention to the bottoms of her feet. Next she did the three-by-three breath work, starting with a deep inhale into her crown. While focusing on the top of her head and holding her breath for three seconds, she tried to sense and feel into both of the labels *nobody* and *somebody* all at once, melting them into each other in her mind and in her body, as one sensation—not as one thought. She then exhaled and discharged the energies of her repressed fears and hidden desires through the bottoms of her feet, into the earth. She repeated this process three times. And with her last exhale, she opened her fists and released the energy she was holding into thin air.

I calmly asked her, "How are you feeling now?"

She was a little teary, yet calm. She almost whispered. "I feel like I have a big realization here. Throughout my life, I've always been angry at people who didn't see me, didn't recognize me, but I now realize that I'm projecting my mom onto them. My annoyance with her had become directed at other people.

"And I have another crazy revelation to share. I now understand why I miss my dad so much. You know, he was the only one, the only person who understood me so well. He was my anchor. He was the one who saw me, recognized me, validated me. Without his validation, I feel angrier, more frustrated with these people who demean and disrespect me. Without my dad's assurance of who I am, I have no support, so I project the anger that I hold against my mom more strongly and aggressively toward others. That's why I miss him even more these days, in these times."

I was impressed by her ability to connect these two separate situations. Indeed, they were related, and they caused polarities in her: one polarity was the achiever who wanted to be recognized, respected, and seen; the other was the nobody who feared being dismissed, demeaned, and disrespected. These opposing forces created an internal conflict that she had been dealing with for decades. And now that she had been able to integrate these polarities, the internal conflict lessened substantially.

She was ready for my next question. "Going forward, how would you like to address a situation in which people demean and disrespect you?"

"Now that my dad is no longer with us, I think I'm the only one who can validate myself. I'm sure that's what he wants for me as well. As long as I feel good about myself, stand up for my own values, and honor my own work, I don't need to turn to others for validation. Going forward, I want to even stand tall in front of my mom. Instead of looking to her for validation, I will just be me: confident, self-assured, sharing—all without asking to be seen."

In just a few sessions, she had dropped off some of her major sandbags. From here on, it was softer, smoother sailing for Frida! She was even more relaxed around her mom, which created space for both of them to lean into each other for comfort and love. It was a wonderful new beginning for both of them, with their connection deepening exponentially into the future.

At work, Frida was surprised that she didn't react as abruptly to the ongoing demeaning, devaluing attitudes or comments from others. After dropping off her sandbags of not being validated or valued, she was able to connect with her own inner power and strength. It was no longer an internal battle or defensive effort to get recognition from other people. Instead, she claimed her own value and sense of being, and she showed up at every meeting and every encounter with higher integrity and presence.

There are hundreds of examples like Frida's, where clarity gracefully flows into consciousness after the integration of repressed fears and hidden desires. My sincere hope is that one day you'll experience this empowering shift in your own consciousness. Afterward you'll find yourself living at a higher level and enjoying deeper awareness and understanding. No words can fully describe how this feels, as the process is unique for each individual. It is a rise in consciousness that only you will get to know and experience.

CHAPTER SIX

REACTING TO TRIGGERS WITH DEFENSIVE SUBCONSCIOUS STRATEGIES

Through the self-discovery work you've done so far, you might have already experienced a consciousness shift, but how would you know if you have? Where are you on the scale of consciousness from 1 to 100?

To find out, all you have to do is observe how you deal with triggers.

When you emotionally *react*, that means you take triggers personally and take defensive actions against them, based on your perceptions or the perceived reality your subconscious internal programming has created. When you react emotionally, you're living within the subconscious realms.

When you *respond*, that means you're aware of your emotions, thoughts, and physical sensations. You're able to ground yourself, take conscious actions, and matter-of-factly respond to your triggers. This capability is only available at self-conscious levels, or what I've called the watchful state.

When you *rise*, that means you're well integrated in your mental, emotional, and physical layers of Self, of your being. You've reached a state of presence where you're not affected by triggers at all, which you can only experience at high-conscious levels.

It's as simple as that.

Now let's explore in more detail specific strategies to discover where you are in the levels of consciousness.

SUBCONSCIOUS DEFENSIVE ACTIONS

When living at a subconscious level, you react to life from two different vantage points: you *defend* your vulnerability and you *cope* with the emotional hurt.

As we've seen, we defend by deploying aggressive, passive-aggressive, or passive defensive actions to ward off the emotional attacks of triggers. When you defend, you know exactly what you are reacting against, and your reactions are visible and noticeable to you and others. For example, you may raise your voice in an argument with your lover, which is an aggressive defensive action; you may gossip about how incompetent your boss is, which is a passive-aggressive defensive action; or you may withdraw from your friends when they disagree with your opinion, a passive defensive action.

What do you do to cope? Coping strategies are more ambiguous. They are mainly your addictions and compulsive behaviors, and you often don't exactly know what you're coping with. Even though you feel the emotional hurt within you, you can't tell what's going on internally. Usually, your coping strategies are part of your daily routine and may not show up as immediate reactions to a trigger the way your defensive actions do.

For example, you may overeat even though you promised yourself the other day not to. Without acknowledging the comfort that junk food offers, you automatically keep going back to food to numb your emotional pain. You may drink to get buzzed in a social gathering without recognizing your social anxiety. You may smoke every night to relax without being aware of what makes you overwhelmed during the day. You may stay late at work without knowing what you're trying to avoid at home. You might even clean your house every day without ever being in touch with your desire to control your environment and people.

We defend and cope for different reasons and under different circumstances. You defend yourself aggressively, for example, when you feel most vulnerable—where your personal power and control is under threat—while at the same time you have some power over the other person or situation that imposes a threat. You believe you can use your power to handle the trigger. You also react aggressively when there's a lot at stake. Aggressive defensive actions include yelling, cursing, blaming, abusing, and overpowering physically or psychologically, and the intensity of these actions is directly proportional to how vulnerable you feel. Your immediate motive is to control and defuse, to make you feel safe and comforted.

When do you use passive-aggressive defensive actions? These actions are used to ward off threats when you don't feel powerful enough to combat them directly. Passive-aggressive actions are therefore indirect and include sarcastic comments, manipulative behavior, gossip, name-calling, eye-rolling, judging others, or doing something behind a person's back to demean or otherwise hurt them. The usual motive in passive-aggressive behavior is revenge, which gives you a sense of relief, equality, safety, and comfort.

What about passive defensive actions? You resort to passive strategies when you feel absolutely powerless against people or situations that challenge and threaten you. In these circumstances, you hold everything in to avoid conflict or run away from the trigger to protect yourself against emotional pain, hurt, and discomfort. Your goal is to build a very thick and tall wall to isolate yourself and create a safer comfort zone.

What is different about coping strategies? They are longer-term strategies than defensive actions. These strategies are always available to you, regardless of any power imbalance between you and the people or situations that trigger you. You can always rely on them to numb your suffering and soothe your emotional pain. With coping strategies, you avoid face-to-face encounters and instead cover up your pain and vulnerability with external resources, by using them in excessive amounts: TV, junk food, alcohol, cigarettes, sex, drugs, gambling, work, exercise, and so on.

Law of Life #21:
Coping strategies serve a purpose.

Coping strategies are neither good nor bad; they're just actions you take to numb your suffering. Like defensive actions, your coping strategies definitely provide you with temporary relief from emotional pain and suffering, until the next limiting life pattern cycle. However, when you engage in these behaviors excessively, you often end up feeling chronically down, depressed, and lost, because they drain your energy and cause physical exhaustion. When they've pulled you deep into the lowest levels of consciousness, you might decide you need to quit the behavior—only to return to it the following day, because neither the self-promises nor the coping strategies address your sandbags.

APPLYING THE POWER METHOD
WHEN TRIGGERED

If you don't want to rely on defensive actions and coping strategies when triggered, because they don't change your subconscious internal programming and therefore you keep experiencing the same limiting life patterns over and over again, then what else is available?

The Rise 2 Realize POWER Method.

You've been studying the Method extensively throughout your journey so far. The time has come to put all that work together to rise in consciousness. At the beginning of every limiting life pattern cycle, at the exact time you're triggered and have an emotional reaction, apply the following steps:

PAUSE to notice and honor your emotions, as provoked by the trigger event.

OBSERVE your thoughts about the person or the situation that set off your emotional reactions.

WELCOME the physical sensations that the emotional reactions created in your body.

EARTH the physical sensations through the three-by-three breath work, exhaling it out of your body and discharging it into the earth through the bottoms of your feet.

RESPOND to the person or the situation by choosing your actions consciously and fully accepting whatever actions you take.

You may wonder how you can embrace defensive actions and coping strategies without self-judgment when those were your chosen reactions. Take a step back and look at your life. Can you criticize the part of your Self that cries for attention? Can you frown upon the part of your Self that yearns for love? How can you put down the part of your Self that desires safety and security? Your goal for now is simply to notice, acknowledge, and accept whatever defensive actions or coping strategies you're using, as well as any tension *they* create in your body, beyond the tension caused by the actual trigger; the goal is not to change the course of your actions, but to learn from them. Practice conscious discomfort more often. Sit with your discomfort without correcting your thoughts or behaviors to become even more self-aware, and to gain even deeper understanding of the part of your Self that craves life.

**Life Skills Assignment #11:
Apply the POWER Method on a daily basis.**

Whenever you have an emotional reaction, stop for a second, take a step back from whatever is happening, apply the steps of the POWER Method, and notice energetic and consciousness shifts within you, if any. At the end of the day, record what happened as part of your daily review.

First, describe the trigger event. Then reflect on how you reacted to it. Maybe you showed your usual reaction, or maybe you reacted differently, in a new way. I included both in our example below for your reference:

The trigger event: Running late to my first appointment in the morning, again!

Describe your usually defensive action: Rushing through traffic, constantly changing lanes, cutting people off, rolling through stop signs.

Describe how you used the POWER Method: This morning, I miraculously remembered to pause when I was rushing through traffic to get to my morning appointment on time. I noticed my anxiety and intense worry. When I took a step back from everything, I observed my thoughts of feeling embarrassed in front of my client: *how can a spiritual mentor, a life coach, regularly run late to his sessions?* Then I dropped into my body and observed the physical tension there. My hands were sweaty. My shoulders were shrugged high, up at ear level, muscles contracted. I took a big breath into my shoulders, held it for three seconds, and released the tension out of my feet into the earth.

Describe how you responded differently: As I was sitting with my discomfort, I started to ask myself why I was rushing. *What's the worst-case scenario? Is it the end of the world that I'm going to be three minutes late?* I observed the next round of thoughts. *I feel embarrassed. I'm not proper. I'm going to be disregarded.* I welcomed those thoughts with another soft breath into my heart, noticing the contraction in my chest, and then I exhaled it out through my feet after a three-second hold. I slowed down the car and came to a full stop at the next stop sign. For the first time in a while, I stayed there for three seconds before I crossed the intersection. As I calmly arrived at my office, I saw my client pull into the parking lot at the same time.

To fully accept that side of your Self that craves comfort and happiness, you need to be both curious and courageous. You need to be very gentle with your Self while looking for answers within about why you do things the way you do. Be warm and welcoming of your different personalities and variations on your conditioned self. At the end of the day, that part that craves happiness and comfort belongs to you and nobody else. Own it. Find out more about it. A whole new integrated you is waiting to be discovered.

Right here! Right now!

CHAPTER SEVEN

RESPONDING TO TRIGGERS WITH ASSERTIVE SELF-CONSCIOUS STRATEGIES

How do you shift away from your subconscious defensive actions and coping strategies to self-conscious responses which allow you to discover more and more of your Self?

Let's review some possible assertive self-conscious strategies to triggers.

DOING THE OPPOSITE

You know by now what to do when triggered. Simply practice the POWER Method and you'll certainly shift your consciousness and the way you respond to a trigger event. Naturally.

That's a given. But how about your conditioned self? What do you do when you observe your conditioned self in action? After all, you're still vulnerable at this level of consciousness. Won't your hidden desires call your conditioned self into action— your perfectionist, people-pleaser, high-achiever self?

As you've seen, there's a tight relationship between the mask you wear and the vulnerability your mask hides. When you climb up the scale of consciousness, your responsibility to live authentically naturally increases. This means you don't want to wear your mask as tightly as before, because your vulnerability is not as painful as you previously felt. You've been healing your old wounds from past experiences. At this level, you know you can't be as much of a perfectionist or a people pleaser anymore, and you don't need to. And that's why it's OK to loosen up your mask a little bit more. How do you do that? By doing the opposite.

You keep chipping small pieces off your mask by *doing the opposite*. There's a moment, called the moment of choice, when you have the opportunity to truly shift your consciousness. When hooked by a trigger in the limiting life pattern cycle, the moment of choice is right before you deploy your defensive actions or engage in a coping strategy or call upon your conditioned self. It's right before you throw the first punch. Right before you take that first sip. Right before you do something to please someone else, if that's what your conditioned self is telling you to do.

In the past, the moment of choice passed by and you didn't have the tools to notice it. Now you can. You can step back and stay with it for a few seconds, hearing the word *no* from your self-conscious, instead of the word *yes* that your subconscious used to whisper, or vice versa.

Law of Life #22:
Life streams in perpetual flow, either
ascending or descending along the scale of
consciousness. Your choice of conscious
action determines the direction.

Let's take a look at some hypothetical examples. Try to picture yourself in them and ask yourself whether you could do the opposite of what you normally might have done in these situations. The purpose of doing the opposite is to step out of your comfort zone, shift your consciousness to a higher level, and observe what happens within you, where you gain different perspectives on the inner workings of your psyche. It challenges your subconscious internal programming, helps you gain deeper insights into your conditioned self, and allows you to play with new ways of embracing limiting life patterns. If you feel any resistance, any tension as you work through these, apply the POWER Method to process the arising emotional reactions, the corresponding repressed fears, and the physical sensations they create in your body.

Here are a few questions to help you practice doing the opposite:

> If you have always made others a priority, can you consciously choose to say *no* to them for once, to carve out some personal time for yourself?

> If you feel uncomfortable being in social situations that lead you to drink a few shots just to

temper your anxiety, can you choose to drink club soda and face your anxiety?

If you have the chance to take on yet another project to impress your boss and increase your visibility in the company—and even heighten the possibility of a promotion—can you stay back and watch one of your colleagues jump on the opportunity?

If you have been a little controlling with your partner and kids lately, can you, just for once, ignore your partner's messiness or your kids' laziness and sit with the discomfort it provokes in you?

If you've been an ambitious hiker, always tracking how far you walk, how high you climb, or how fast you can complete the loop, can you go on your next hike to enjoy every step and notice surrounding nature? Can you avoid glancing at your phone or watch to check the time?

If you have been anxious and worried about where your long-term relationship is going because your partner doesn't seem to have the same level of commitment and closeness as you do, can you, instead of questioning them about your future together, choose to back off and just be present each day, demonstrating your love without agenda or expectation?

If you have difficulty focusing on what you need to get done and keep finding yourself bingeing on Netflix or scrolling down social media feeds, can you commit to staying present with your original task for fifteen minutes at a time, riding out the urge to walk away and facing the pressure and itchiness to quit?

If usually you are the one who listens to your friend's problems and plays the fixer and helper, always winding up depleted after you meet with them, can you share some of yourself with them in your next meetup and openly tell them about *your* life? In other words, can you ask them to listen to you?

If you have been a social butterfly and love to be the center of attention wherever you go, can you skip a party or two, and attempt to do something without any company, or stand quietly in the corner and observe others at the next party that you attend?

The point of this doing-the-opposite strategy is to learn how to counteract the opposing forces of repressed fears and hidden desires. Remember, the pendulum swings between the polar opposite forces of repressed fears and hidden desires. When you're about to swing toward perfectionist, people pleaser, high achiever, and so on—which are your conditioned selves operating from hidden desires—you need to do the opposite to swing back to neutral territory. If a trigger ignites your repressed fears, when your defensive actions normally come into play or your coping strategies become active again, can you then challenge them in order to neutralize the force that pulls you off center?

Every year, I go back to Turkey to visit my family. One of these visits occurred when I was experimenting with doing the opposite. As you know by now, I was the epitome of a people pleaser. That summer, though, I had a big mission: I was going to reclaim my self-boundaries.

My parents arranged a beautiful trip to Marmaris, a gorgeous vacation town in southern Turkey on the crystal clear Mediterranean Sea. I was grateful to my parents for doing this for me and I was loving every minute of it, but I also had to execute my doing-the-opposite plan out of respect for my Self. One late afternoon, my dad and I were hanging out at a local bar close to our hotel. The bartender announced that it was happy hour and stood ready to take our drink orders. In Turkey, it's tradition that father and son drink raki to bond. My dad ordered his glass of raki right away. The bartender turned to me and was ready to type "two" on his order sheet. Wanting to practice doing the opposite and to set my boundaries, I asked for hot tea instead.

The opportunity presented itself out of the blue. I didn't plan for it to happen at a certain time or in a certain way. My intention was there, and it happened. Of course, the effect was significant for me. I immediately felt the emotional shock waves of saying something different from what was expected of me. I was finally standing up for myself, yet I felt extremely uncomfortable with the unchartered waters I was entering into, which I hadn't been in my entire life. I felt empowered that I was building my self-boundaries. My response wasn't a reaction to a trigger, but an attempt to establish my personal freedom. As a result, I felt I could finally breathe a little.

I remember another doing-the-opposite opportunity, this time with my mom. It was a different summer trip to Turkey, and we were all going to my nephew's wedding reception.

Everyone was supposed to dress nicely, but I hadn't brought anything other than my blue jeans and checkered shirt. Though not high-end, they were nonetheless designer items, and they were what I'd been planning to wear. And I did— despite knowing my mom would disapprove of my attire and be very disappointed with my choice. I felt that I was finally my own person!

From your past experiences, you may think that standing up for yourself means getting blowback, which, of course, leads to another trigger that will drag you down to where you were before. The doing-the-opposite strategy is only available to you after you have done some integration of your repressed fears and hidden desires and have a sense of presence. Until then, any attempts may yield further conflicts. To avoid any misunderstanding—you're not applying the doing-the-opposite strategy to gain power, but you're taking this step because you already feel a natural presence or inner feeling to expand your self-boundaries.

Therefore, if you're simultaneously doing the opposite and cringing about what the other person will think of you, then you're still at a lower level of consciousness and subject to intense and frequent triggers. As a result, your actions will not be assertive enough and will attract a negative reaction from the other person. When you are at a self-conscious level and have processed some portion of your repressed fears through integration, you don't get blowback as easily as you would have in lower consciousness levels. If you do, it means you haven't processed your fears as well as you thought. No big deal. You can go back and process that trigger resulting from the blowback and see how others' reactions affected you and your body. After additional processing, when you try again at the next opportunity to test where you are on the scale of consciousness, there's a higher chance that you'll be successful in your experiment with doing the opposite. In that case, you will experience much softer blowback, if any, indicating higher levels of consciousness.

Another important note is that I was doing the opposite not to hurt my parents or plot revenge against them. It's not a tactic to overpower others or dismiss their presence or disrespect their character. At higher consciousness levels, power is used to create presence, not to get into power games with others—which is defensive and results in depletion of your energy and theirs. On the contrary, as I felt more grounded and centered with my doing-the-opposite action, I was grateful for my parents and for everything they've done for me, not just for those summers when they hosted me in Turkey, but throughout my life. In fact, the more I discover my Self, the better I understand them.

Therefore, when we get to our assertive self-conscious strategies, it's really about *us*, not about others. At this level, we accept whatever happened in the past and then express it in such ways that allow us to gain our self-respect, self-worth, and power back—not from other people, but from within ourselves. And for ourselves.

Life Skills Assignment #12:
Do the opposite when responding to triggers.

Now it's your turn. How do you think you'll feel when you have to make these conscious choices that are different than previous choices you've made? You probably know the answer already. Most likely, you will feel overwhelmed, horrified, even nauseated. Doing the opposite to face your vulnerability is not a child's game. Yet it is one of the most effective strategies to drop off your sandbags. Suggesting you do something different than before, and inviting you to override your fight-or-flight operating system, is like asking you to jump off a cliff. Initially, you feel unsafe. You are totally out of your comfort zone. On the other hand, Life doesn't want you to hurt yourself. What if you're actually holding on to a hang glider or you grow imaginary wings that lift you up, the moment you jump off? When you apply the doing-the-opposite strategy with a conscious intention of facing your fears and desires, you gain altitude, a new perspective. You drop your sandbags, feel lighter, and naturally rise to higher altitudes, where you have access to better views of life.

What do you think will happen when you step out of your comfort zone, leave your village behind, face the dragon, and venture through and beyond the forest? How will you feel when you break free from the captivity of your subconscious internal programming? Be forewarned: in addition to feeling scared, you might also initially feel guilt. Or shame. Or social awkwardness, isolation, or judgment from others. Will this be OK with you? Are you ready to become unstuck? With all this work under your belt so far, and the ability to access the grounding energies of the earth whenever you need to, you'll be able to accomplish anything you set your sights on. As you start to sense already, you are slowly taking charge of your life. Can you taste your individual freedom and newfound emotional mastery? Do you feel that new sense of presence surrounding you, within you?

Here's another personal experience, with specific items to note when applying the doing-the-opposite strategy to your triggers:

> *Describe the trigger event:* The person in front of me is taking too much time at the cashier.

Describe how you used the POWER Method: As soon as I felt my impatience rushing up to my head, like fire, I felt a lump in my throat, as if I wanted to scream at the person. I paused and observed my impatient thoughts and inhaled into the pressure I felt in my throat. I held my breath for three seconds, and then I exhaled and released the physical charge to the earth. I did this two more times. After my three-by-three breath work, I turned my focus on the bottoms of my feet to connect with the earth and felt some calmness coming over me.

Apply doing the opposite: Instead of rolling my eyes and turning to the person behind me to passively criticize the slow patron, which I usually do, I was able to collect myself and back up a few steps to give more space to them. That's when I realized he was actually rushing to get everything out of his shopping basket and onto the counter. Feeling a sense of empathy for his nervous rush, I said, "Please take your time!"

Describe how the other person responded or how the situation shifted: He turned around and thanked me, appearing relieved. He smiled. I'd never had this kind of interaction at the grocery store before, and I felt surprisingly joyful inside. I smiled back at him. He completed his transaction and left a few minutes later.

When you sit down tonight to write in your daily review journal, record how this practice worked or did not work out for you. Pay special attention to how it made you feel and whether you were surprised by the outcome of your changed response to a trigger and how others responded to you.

Law of Life #23:
Life becomes magical when you ride the wave of unpredictability with curiosity.

Well, if you still get overwhelmed, you now know what to do! You can run the POWER Method; WELCOME the emotional charge by inhaling into the physical sensations that arise in your body from doing the opposite, and then discharge it with a strong exhale into the earth. Stay curious.

By the way, if you can't do the opposite and you are not ready to consciously face your discomfort, it's OK! Don't force it. Be patient. Give yourself some time to practice more self-observation. Look over your notes in your daily reviews. Get in touch with early memories, origins of your repressed fears, to understand more about your subconscious internal programming. Trust me, life will bring endless opportunities for you to practice. If you miss one, you'll get another chance soon. Remember you are trying to get out of your comfort zone by only one inch at a time, not by a foot or a mile. Be curious and experiment with it each time.

USING I-STATEMENTS

Subconscious internal programming makes us all live in fear—rightfully so, as it interprets the situations that are happening today as *threats* according to the painful experiences that happened in the past. This living-in-fear state makes us pay attention to the outside world, to whatever is happening outside of ourselves. That's why we develop our unique, individual survival mechanisms—our defensive actions, coping strategies, and conditioned self.

But when we direct our attention outward to survive, we don't know what's going on inside of us. We don't know why we emotionally react or why we're addicted to this or that. We also don't know why we chase success or why we give up ourselves to meet the need of others.

Through the self-observation practice, you've started to learn how to split your attention between outside and inside. As a result, you've accessed higher consciousness levels and become aware of what's going on in your head. Now the time has come to share it with the world by using I-statements. These statements are basically reflections of feelings that you have in your mind and heart, feelings that you haven't dared to share with others before. They are your own proprietary information and have nothing to do with others. Even though others may have triggered you, the I-statement, as an assertive self-conscious strategy, reminds you to focus on your Self, and your feelings, without expecting a certain outcome from anyone else. At this level, your consciousness is high enough to be able to use I-statements to express your feelings matter-of-factly rather than defensively. What you are about to share is what's really going on with you, within you. That's all. Only your feelings and thoughts. Nothing else. I-statements are great tools to establish healthy boundaries in all relationships. After all, the power is not how well you can hide your weaknesses, but the extent to which you can accept, acknowledge, and welcome them.

Law of Life #24:
Whatever is repressed needs to be expressed.

When do you use I-statements? Right before you deploy your defensive actions to ward off a trigger. Instead of going with your usual reactions, first PAUSE to notice your emotions and OBSERVE your thoughts, and then you're ready to use your I-statements.

The timing might even be *as* you notice them happening to you:

> "I'm getting angry right now."
> "I feel a little frustrated here."
> "I'm sad, you know?"

Don't be shy about sharing your feelings. Tell others what's going on in your mind *and* in your heart:

> "I felt put down by that statement."
> "I felt less-than when I heard those words."
> "I felt dismissed when I didn't hear back."

As you're still in transition from subconscious to self-conscious levels, your I-statements may come out sounding defensive at first. You will know how they sound by observing how others react. Do they get defensive and start arguing with you? Does their facial expression, body language, or tone of voice shift? If so, you may want to try using another I-statement, again solely focusing on *your* feelings, to diffuse the tension. Whenever you are on defense, it feels like an offense to the other person. Whenever they're on defense, it feels like an offense to you. That's why we experience entangle-ments in relationships in which each partner puts the other on defense, and they keep offending each other in never-ending arguments.

While sharing your I-statements, remember that your feel-ings are not negotiable. Your feelings belong to you. No one can argue you out of them, although they might sometimes try. They might say you're too sensitive, too soft, or making a big deal out of nothing. They might say you shouldn't have felt that way. They might switch tactics and try to intimidate you. The answer to them is an easy one: "My feelings are not negotiable. That's how I feel. And yes, I am sensitive." Own them. Express them—freely, assertively, and matter-of-factly.

Law of Life #25
Feelings are not negotiable.

I-statements are important, and effective, because there is no *you* in them. Why not? Because using the word *you* creates a defensive stance against others. When you say, "I feel this way because you did that," it puts the blame on the person who triggered you, and it doesn't emphasize *your* feelings. The main purpose of I-statements is to establish your self-boundaries. When someone triggers you, they usually cross your bound-aries and take your power away—or, alternatively, you *give* your power away. Your initial instinctive reaction is to kick the triggering individuals out of your space, back to where they belong, by pointing the finger at them. And the moment you say *you*, they think you are blaming them, which feels like an attack or threat to them, even though they might have been the ones who attacked you first.

When you use the defensive *you*-statement, you are basically counterattacking and letting them know that they've invaded your personal territory. But now you're doing the same, crossing *their* boundaries. You're putting them into a position where they will want to defend themselves, and they'll launch their own counterattack. And this power game goes on and on, back and forth, until one of you gives up. That's why arguments, especially within couples, can go for hours—or even longer—without anyone really knowing how it all started, with each person trying to establish power over the other, or at least trying to retain their own boundaries.

I remember one spring morning in my last corporate job, I was in a meeting with my boss, and we were reviewing another presentation we were about to give to the board of directors. When we got to a section in the presentation where we both realized that I'd missed a big data point, he suddenly got upset with me and abruptly left the meeting.

I was devastated. I was so upset and depleted that I couldn't run after him, as my usual people-pleaser self would, to call him back to the conference room to continue. I couldn't sleep that night; I was so angry at him, even though I'd done enough transformation work by then to know that my repressed fears of abandonment, betrayal, and dismissal had all been triggered. I knew this wasn't about him. It was about me—and my own sandbags. But I still kept blaming him for being so condescending that he would just walk out on me. The more defensive I got, and the more I focused on what he did, the more hooked into my limiting life pattern cycle I became. Running through that vicious cycle, I kept ending up in that same old conflict/confusion state. *I can't stand this place. I don't think I can stay here for even one more month. I should quit tomorrow!*

The following day, I decided to face the situation head-on. I'd been practicing I-statements around this time, so I thought it would be an opportunity to sharpen my life skills. I invited

him to a one-on-one meeting in a different conference room—
not the one we were in before—and I told him how I had felt
the day before when he abruptly left the meeting.

"Yesterday I felt left alone in the meeting. I was very upset
when our meeting got interrupted, and I felt that our trust was
broken. I feel that if we want to work together in the future,
we need to stick with each other and understand where each
one of us is coming from. If we could do that, I feel like we
can establish a strong partnership and make working together
more fun. What do you think?"

I didn't rehearse any of this beforehand. I couldn't believe
what was coming out of my mouth. My body was slightly shaking with nervousness. And as I talked, I also felt a little sadness.
I was remembering other times when I'd felt abandoned and
dismissed, and I hadn't been able to say anything or express
my feelings. Whatever was locked inside of me was now coming out here, with my boss. After the meeting, we shook hands.
I felt a sense of relief, and I never looked back at this incident
with defensive eyes. In fact, our relationship got even better
over the coming months until I left the corporate world, about
eighteen months later, forever.

Now think about where you might use I-statements in your
life. Imagine, for example, what might normally happen if you
accused your partner of paying more attention to their phone
than to you all night long. Of course, they'd feel attacked. They
might also be offended or disagree with you. They'd certainly
get defensive and might even launch a counterattack, accusing you of things you could do better. Does anyone ever win
these arguments? The blame game sometimes goes back-and-
forth for hours until you've each become exhausted, and you
might not even remember what started the argument in the
first place.

Now imagine a different conversation, one in which you
speak your truth. What do you really want at the dinner table?

You want to feel a true connection with your partner. So share an I-statement.

"I felt dismissed when we didn't connect with each other at dinner." You're telling your partner exactly how you feel. There's no need or room to negotiate. Do you see the difference? Do you sense the gentler tone?

You might even say there's no need to respond. "I just wanted to let you know. You can do whatever you want with this information. You don't need to change for me. You can even keep looking at your phone during our next dinner. But, if you do, just know that I'll feel dismissed. And I'm happy to share with you why I do. That's all! Thanks, babe!"

One important point, though. While sharing your feelings, you can't use them to manipulate others, or change them, or turn them into a different person who will please you and not trigger you. You can't ask them to do things just so that you are happy. This could be a temptation when you're still living at the subconscious level, but the good news is that, once you achieve self-conscious levels, you won't care to manipulate others, as you feel more and more grounded and centered. At this level, you don't get attached to other people's behaviors and how they trigger you. At this level, you're striving for equality, your fair share of personal boundaries, interdependent and harmonious existence, and graceful flow.

If you do want the other person to change, and it's OK if you do, then keep in mind that might risk creating the sort of codependency that often plagues long-term relationships. By asking another person to change, you might inadvertently create a mutually defensive tit-for-tat relationship. *If you change, I'll do this for you, and if I change, I want you to do this for me.* This transactional bargaining agreement eventually makes couples codependent on each other for their happiness, and over time it entangles the flow of their relationship, leading both of them to stagnancy, rather than to openness and spontaneity.

In addition, this self-imposed defensive codependency tilts the power dynamic within the couple. *If you do this for me, only then can I love you.* This codependency shift can create a seesaw pattern, where you and your partner start building up resentment against each other as you do specific things to earn conditional love. You are at one another's mercy, waiting for love. Over time, this built-up resentment will show up in even more arguments and disagreements between you, and you'll each deploy more and more defensive actions in an attempt to take back individual control and destroy this codependent structure.

Of course, all these defensive actions are happening at the subconscious level. No one is getting up in the morning and conspiring to hurt or overpower their partner. You're both just defending yourselves in your own perceived realities, whatever they may be shaped by: fear of abandonment, rejection, or betrayal; of being not good enough, not valued, not appreciated, and so on. And as you do, you're becoming even more dependent on the conditional love that you've been promised.

But if you try to use I-statements without manipulation or power games, and instead with a grounded, centered, and neutral mindset, and you state the facts as you see them, you'll be able to create healthy boundaries and stay in your own lane. You'll let your partner be who they are and avoid stepping across their boundaries. You'll learn to respect your *own* feelings as well as theirs, because they're entitled to their feelings as much as you are to yours.

> **Life Skills Assignment #13:**
> **Use I-statements when responding**
> **to triggers, and share your feelings**
> **matter-of-factly with others.**

Notice how you used an I-statement during a trigger event when you sit down to write in your daily review journal. Here's an example for your reference:

> *Describe the trigger event:* My significant other asked me to take on yet another house project on top of everything else I'm doing around the house. I thought, *A typical move by my partner!* I got annoyed and felt criticized for not doing enough for my family. I felt that she was pressuring me to do something to be worthy of her love.
>
> *Describe how you used the POWER Method:* I resented that I wasn't being recognized for all the things I already do around the house. I wanted to scream at my partner, but this time instead of raising my voice, I remembered to pause. I observed what was going through my head, and then I was able to drop into my body. Thank God, I had been doing my self-observation meditation regularly for the last couple of weeks. Now I felt that sense of space again and was more connected with the physical sensations in my body. I found a huge lump of tension in my throat. I inhaled and exhaled into

the earth and ran through the standard three-by-three breath work.

Describe how you used I-statements to create your boundaries: I was feeling a little more grounded so I decided to use I-statements. "I'm a little annoyed right now, honey. I feel some kind of pressure that I always need to do something around the house in order to get your attention, get your recognition, get your love. I'd love to know more about how you see me. Do you feel that I'm failing to meet your expectations?"

Describe how you felt after using I-statements: Phew! I felt so good, so relieved. I realized I'd been holding so much inside. Instead of using my usual aggressive defensive actions of blaming my partner, I was able to express what was going on inside of *me*, and I was also able to ask her how she felt about me and the situation we are in. For some strange reason, I felt calm after the initial nervousness, right when I started expressing my I-statement. I was a little worried in the beginning, but once I got going with the intention of expressing myself, everything felt natural. I was also surprised that I became curious about my partner's point of view.

Describe how the other person responded or how the situation shifted: When I realized that I used *you* in my I-statement, I got a little nervous that it wasn't going to work out. Yet

I was genuinely curious about what she really thought about me, so the question just came out like that. And it worked! I was shocked that it did! As soon as I shared my feelings openly, my partner was very receptive to what I had to say, and we got into an incredibly intimate conversation about our fears and what we could do to express them. My partner was also able to express her fears of not being appreciated and not being valued if we don't attend to things around the house and create beautiful, harmonious, and loving living conditions together. I felt so close to her and realized, maybe for the first time in our relationship, that deep down we want the same things.

HONORING YOUR HEART VALUES

What are heart values?

First, let's define what a value is. It's a concept, a thought, a belief, a mission, or a point of view on life that is important and meaningful to you. Your values are, in a sense, the motor that sets you into perpetual movement in life. They motivate you to behave in accordance with what's important to you. No matter what happens, you practically always live according to your values.

The key question becomes this: What values do *you* live by?

In order to gain deeper understanding, you need to separate them into two categories: mind values and heart values.

Mind values are basically the thought patterns and belief systems we've reviewed previously—the values that arise from your subconscious internal programming. They are the survival-based values that stem from your repressed fears and hidden desires. When you operate at the subconscious level, you pretty much live according to your mind values. For example, I thought and believed that I needed to conform in order to avoid conflict. I needed to be proper and put together to feel in control. I needed to become an accountant to feel financially secure. I needed to be nice to be liked, and I needed to withdraw to protect myself from embarrassment or mockery. I also needed to work harder to achieve, stay quiet to be accepted and included, and join groups to avoid being lonely.

Heart values, on the other hand, arise from your real nature, your true essence. Generally, your mind values suppress your heart values while you're growing up, as you learn how to go about life and hedge the risks of an unknown, unpredictable future. By the time you're an adult, your heart values become clearer and want to be recognized and acted upon. For example, going on walks to feel connected with nature, and with my Self, became important to me. Traveling to foreign countries to experience different cultures opened my eyes to the people of the world. Dancing gave me energetic physical expansion as I experienced my body moving to music. Biking made me feel the wind on my face and a sense of freedom. Writing poetry opened my inner world as I watched the words flow through my hands. Spending time with friends offered deep connections that instilled joy. Being of service to others and helping people experience their highest potential brought fulfillment and meaning to my life.

How can you find out about your heart values and connect with them?

Through trial and error. Heart values naturally appear as inclinations as you rise in consciousness. In order to connect with them, be open and curious. Experiment with life. This means consciously exploring life and finding out what you like and don't like about each experience. You have your entire life to discover your Self, and new opportunities continuously surface to help you. Every life experience can serve as a teaching moment for you to understand your Self deeper.

You can start by listening to your inner feelings and sensing what you enjoy and what you don't. As you practice inward attention, the connection with your inner feelings, with those inclinations, will strengthen, and you will be able to notice more specifically what you liked about a particular experience and what you didn't. This isn't about making up some kind of surface-level mental construct concerning how you felt, but instead about exploring your inner feelings and letting your passion, connection, and deeper sense of truth guide you toward your heart values.

Another way to discover your heart values is to listen to your complaints. When you are not happy with a situation, that usually means you're not honoring one of your heart values. Ask yourself why you're complaining.

> You are not happy with your relationship.
> Why not?
>
> You are not happy with your current job.
> Why not?
>
> You are not happy with your car.
> Why not?

Without finger-pointing at others for their wrongdoings, bring your attention inward and understand *your* preferences. What matters to you? What's important in life? What makes your heart beat faster? I spent nearly twenty years in the world of accounting and finance. In the first week of my career, as an auditor at one of the Big Six accounting firms, I found myself in despair. I didn't know what to do. The firm's training was superb; I knew I was technically ready to go into the field and do my job. But I didn't feel connected to the work, and I thought I'd made a big mistake with my career choice. I thought I should have been in another field—maybe marketing, or maybe psychology. As time went on, even though my colleagues loved working with me, all the partners praised my work, and I had a great relationship with my clients, I still felt something was missing in me.

Despite this feeling, during each and every day of the nineteen years and five months I spent in the corporate world, I showed up at work to diligently honor my mind values:

> *Financial security:* I chose a stable career that is always in demand.

> *Career advancement:* I chose a profession that presented a bright future to me.

> *Predictability, stability:* My jobs offered clear promotion paths. The hard work always paid off.

I also honored some of my heart values:

> *Working with people:* As a chartered accountant, I worked on various teams and with a variety of clients. In high tech, I worked with people in different departments with various backgrounds, interests, and personality styles.

> *Flexibility:* Because the workload was seasonal, I had time to weave personal interests into my life.

> *Using analytical skills:* I used my analytical and investigative skills to be a proficient auditor,

effective controller, and successful vice president of finance.

Tight deadlines, pressure to work overtime, client or corporate demands, and juggling too many concurrent projects
were among my complaints about these jobs. Everyone com-
plained about these problems. But then one day, I found myself
complaining about something I didn't hear from anybody
else. *What I'm doing here does not contribute to the world at
large.* Once I acknowledged my complaint, that inner voice
grew louder and stronger. I'd hear it every morning when I left
home for work and every night when I came back. *What you
are doing doesn't help others or lift the collective spirit of the
world.* I didn't know what exactly I was supposed to do, but one
thing was clear: I was not honoring one of my top heart values:
service to others.

**Law of Life #26:
Life leads you along an exploratory path
intrinsically aligned with your values.**

I immediately started looking at opportunities to honor my
heart values. I became a certified personal trainer, but it wasn't
sufficiently empowering for my clients, so I stopped. I wondered about joining a suicide hotline team at the American
Red Cross, but I felt I was already too stressed and anxious at
my day job and answering suicide calls would be too much for
me to handle. Finally, I attended a few meetings at a local Big
Brothers Big Sisters organization. I loved it, but I wanted to
have an even bigger impact.

Without quitting my corporate job cold turkey, I continued to experience life, explore alternatives, and knock on a few doors. I followed my inclinations and kept searching, journeying through many trials and errors. Each time, I tuned in to my inner feeling, my inner knowing. *Do I like this? Why? Why not?*

And then the day came when I finally found a calling that matched my heart value of service to others: life coaching and spiritual mentoring. Interestingly, what I do now honors my other heart values as well: meeting new people, analyzing their lives, decoding their internal programming, observing and comparing their journeys before and after, exploring the complex structures of limiting life patterns, and investigating and auditing the System of Life.

Your path is the same in terms of actualizing your Self and realizing your dreams, whatever your calling might be: a loving, caring parent; a deeply connected friend; an inspiring teacher; a successful entrepreneur; a creative designer or builder or painter; or maybe a genius engineer. Your heart values don't need to include service to others, and you may not know right away what they are. Not to worry: your heart values will keep pulling you in the right direction. Stay on your path, in your own lane, and try to keep walking forward as you closely follow your inclinations.

As you listen to this pull and to these invitations, you'll eventually find a unique path to connect with your calling and realize your highest potential. The keys to making this connection include remaining curious about who you are, being aware of your complaints, and understanding the root cause of your dissatisfaction in whatever situation you find yourself. Then, and only then, you begin to courageously explore what life has to offer, not only where you are right now, but also beyond, into the future.

> **Life Skills Assignment #14:**
> **Discover your heart values and explore**
> **new steps to honor them, to inch your**
> **way out of your comfort zone.**

Do you remember the life evaluation form you completed at the beginning of your journey of self-discovery? It would be a good idea to go back and reassess your life from the perspective of your current level of consciousness. When you do, pick an area of your life from the form and create two lists: what you like about it and what you don't like about it. Then ask yourself what's missing from your life, what your complaints are, which heart values are being ignored, and what specific actions you might want to take to honor those missing heart values.

For your reference, let's review the following example about discovering heart values in your career.

> *Describe your primary complaint:* I don't feel fulfilled in my career anymore. Every morning I drag myself out of bed and hardly find the energy to do anything during the day at work. Very unmotivated and uninspired.
>
> *What is missing in that area of your life?* Excitement. I don't like being locked in the office and following monotonous schedules. I'm fed up with routines designed to accomplish tasks for the company, for someone else. I wish I could be out in nature, doing things with my hands, interacting with others, with different people.

What are your heart values? Being out and about, having flexibility in my schedule, connecting with nature, working with my hands, meeting new people, doing things for myself.

What specific and measurable actions would you like to take to honor these heart values in your life? When I take a step back from everything and look at what I feel like doing, certain occupations come to my mind, not as an immediate career choice, but as a way of living. Initially, because it's an exploratory phase, I don't want to get hung up on a specific goal that my mind might have influence over. I don't want to just quit and pursue my heart values impulsively. That would be a defensive action. I would probably end up attracting the same complaints into my life as limiting life patterns. I want to keep my mind open, my options versatile, so that I feel a sense of greater possibility in my explorations.

Maybe I can join the botanical garden volunteers. Maybe I can visit a woodcarving workshop or ceramic atelier nearby. Maybe I can just start taking some walks in the state park and bring my camera with me—the camera that has been sitting around for the last couple of years. What's the easiest step that I can take today? OK, the nature walk and taking some pictures seem to be easy to do. When? This weekend. On Saturday. Where? In Woodside.

The point of this assignment is to practice connecting with your curiosity and spontaneity while exploring your life to discover your heart values, instead of passively complaining and creating stagnancy. You're learning to be guided by your inclinations and inner feelings, practicing being true to your own heart values, to your essence.

You can repeat this exercise for other areas on your life evaluation form: health, relationships, friends, family, and so on. Whether or not these exercises involve practicing conversations with other people or examining your inner dialogue, the assignment remains the same—to discover your heart values, learn to inch your way out of your restrictive comfort zone, and create the life that reflects your true nature, which eventually leads you to your highest potential, Ultimate Happiness.

Here are some additional examples to help you with your assignment.

> Let's say you want to date. Why do you want to date? Do you want to find someone to share life with, or do you want someone to keep you company? What kind of person would you like to date? Why her? Why him? Do you have any particular interests, ideas, feelings, or life visions that connect you more deeply with particular people?

> Let's say you want to break up. Why do you want to leave this relationship? Do you deserve better? Why? What don't you like about this relationship? What is your ideal relationship? What kind of relationship will make you feel fulfilled, seen, heard? What kind of person would you like to be with in your ideal relationship? How do your heart values match your relationship ideals?

Let's say you're trying to get promoted. Why do you want that promotion? Do you want to make more money? Do you want to expand the size of your team so you feel more self-worth and importance? Do you want to work on different projects and connect with new people to enhance your career? In other words, how does a promotion reflect your true essence?

Let's say you start a philanthropic venture or form a nonprofit. Why that area? Do you do it because it feels cool to run a nonprofit in a field that everyone is interested in, or because you feel deeply passionate about the cause and you have some original ideas that you'd like to share with others? What heart value are you trying to fulfill?

You can discover your heart values even when buying a car. What kind of car? Why that car? Do you buy it because everyone says it's a great car, or because it gives you a certain aura, certain status, certain look, or certain appeal? How do you like the feeling of being in that particular car? How does it drive around the curves? In general, how does it feel to drive it? Which car connects with your inner passion? Which car, what design, which brand truly reflects your essence?

Can you see the subtle differences between possible mind values and possible heart values in these examples? Have you started to discern the differences in your own life? Your individual experiences will tell you over time who you are and what's important to you. If you are living mostly subject to your mind values, you'll feel more reactionary. The connection with what you do and what you have will not be as deep and harmonious. Your life will feel contracted and limited. But as you slowly rise in consciousness levels and connect more with your heart values, you'll experience a sense of ease and flow, and satisfaction and fulfillment will permeate your life.

CHAPTER EIGHT

RISING ABOVE TRIGGERS WITH INTEGRATIVE HIGH-CONSCIOUS STRATEGIES

You've been training and learning how to rise above subconscious internal programming to realize your highest potential, Ultimate Happiness, the flow state that leads toward a life of joy, love, abundance, fulfillment, and meaning. Now you have come to a point at which your efforts to rise will no longer require as much of your energy as they did in the lower consciousness levels. Yet you can still develop certain skillsets and a variety of strategies to create that flow state and connect with life in a deeper and more meaningful way.

Now you're about to shift gears to a higher level. The following high-conscious strategies involve your attention split fifty-fifty: half of your attention goes to the outside, on the other person or situation, and half of your attention remains on your Self and what's going on inside. Employing these strategies will further transcend the repressed fears and hidden desires and help you travel further on your journey of self-discovery toward Ultimate Happiness.

HOLDING SPACE: CONSCIOUS LISTENING WITH CURIOSITY

When you're operating under your subconscious internal programming, your attention is fully outward, on people and what they're doing to you. You constantly stay defensive, wanting to ward off perceived threats to your vulnerability, and as a result you get stuck in the same patterns over and over.

When you get to the self-conscious levels, you've developed a deeper awareness and understanding of your Self, and your attention is completely, one hundred percent, inward. Even though you interact with others as you go about your life, your focus remains on your Self; as a result, you find yourself less and less stuck.

Now, at the high-conscious level, you no longer need to defend your vulnerability. You can afford to hold space for others as they express themselves, their Self, to you. You can consciously listen to them with curiosity as you try to understand where they're coming from, what their defenses and fears might be, and the source of their perceived realities, not to judge them—you've been there, you know, you understand— but to help create mutual growth and connection with each other.

Imagine you're leaning toward someone to hear them better, your face in that attentive, curious state as you try to understand what they are saying. In another situation, imagine meeting your best friend after months of being away from each other. You see them and you hold your arms wide open, with a smile on your face, to welcome them. Now combine the feelings of these two situations. Can you feel both the curiosity and the joy together? That's how conscious listening with curiosity feels. It naturally invites you to hold space for others without judgment, without trying to fix them, without trying to make them feel better, without labeling their reaction or situation, without controlling their emotions or how they feel. It's just being there with open arms, welcoming them into that space for sharing emotions and feelings.

Everyone has repressed fears and hidden desires. Everyone wants to be heard, wants to be seen, wants to be understood, and wants to belong as much as you do. Can you consciously listen to them? You'll be able to now, at this high level of consciousness. You've released some of your sandbags. You've lightened the weight of life on your shoulders. But you must still beware the urge to interrupt someone when they're talking, when they're sharing their hurt feelings, when they're blaming you. Watch out for any tendency to fix their problems or too quickly apologize for your mistakes. They may be asking for an apology, but they also might just be asking to be heard, to be seen, to be held. Can you now listen to others without imposing your own agenda or forcing your point of view? Can you simply hold space for them with deep, sincere curiosity?

At this high-conscious level, you'll find it easier to access that curiosity. Don't worry if you can't initially; it will become more and more natural for you to actively and attentively listen from your own journey's perspective. You'll know roughly where others are in their lives, what consciousness levels they're at, what they're going through, where they are coming from, or what their repressed fears and hidden desires might be. You'll now better understand their motives, as well as their survival mechanisms. You will start to see them as a reflection of your Self. There will, of course, still be times when you are confused or don't understand something; in those situations, you might ask them *why?* and *what if?* to invite them to open up and maybe even to conduct their own internal investigations.

I remember the days when I was anxious and nervous about making a point in conversations with others. I would often interrupt at the wrong time to share my opinions and thoughts. Even when interacting one-on-one, I would always be thinking about what I was going to say instead of listening to what the other person was saying. But as I slowly turned my attention inward, I realized my hidden desire to be recognized. I had been selfishly trying to satisfy that desire by getting attention with my smart comments so that I would feel good about myself. Nowadays, as I try to step back from that tendency to seek recognition, which still creeps into my thoughts and actions from time to time, I feel so much richer inside. I can listen to someone talk about themselves and my curiosity about them enriches my life; I now see them as a reflection of me.

**Life Skills Assignment #15:
Hold space for someone, and consciously
listen with curiosity to what they're sharing.**

Find an opportunity to practice this assignment with your partner, your kids, your parents, your boss, your colleagues, or your friends. It might be when a trigger threatens your vulnerability, or it might be a new conversation you initiate. You might prompt an intimate interaction with an open-ended question. You might share an experience you just had involving a topic of mutual interest to create an exchange of ideas. After your prompt, stop and wait for the other person to talk. When you find yourself wanting to jump in to share your thoughts, or correct theirs, hold yourself back. Notice the silence and how uncomfortable it feels. Maybe even try to tune into the place in your body where you can feel that discomfort. Can you hold space? Can you listen? Can you learn more about the person you are speaking with?

Here's a typical scenario to give you some ideas. As usual, record the situation in your daily review.

> *Describe the trigger event:* Here we go again. My partner comes home from work, and without even saying hi, she gets into complaining mode about how things are run at her company. Numerous times, I have told her to quit her job and find another one, but nope, she likes what she does, even though she can't stand her boss, who also happens to be the CEO. I'm really fed up with her complaints, especially right when she comes home and we're about to chill and prepare a nice dinner together. I have a stressful job too, but I usually keep things to myself. I don't want to share my complaints with her because I don't want to further upset her.

> *Describe how you felt when you tried to hold space and consciously listen:* I usually try to calm her down and find solutions for her problems. This time, instead of telling her to quit, I suggested she talk to her HR department. I said she should "see what they have to say about your boss's micromanaging, borderline-abusive behavior." Right after I said it, I realized that I was being my "fixer" and "caregiver" conditioned selves. I immediately applied the POWER Method, and afterward I felt centered

and grounded. I was able to acknowledge to myself that I was trying to make her happy even though it's not my job to fix her situation. What I *can* do is hold space for her and try to understand her complaints by consciously listening. While focusing on connecting to the earth through my feet, I started asking some questions about how she felt or what she thought her boss's intent might be. To my surprise, I felt calmer and more connected with her. I realized more and more what makes her so amazing: the way she thinks, the way she tackles difficulties at work, and how resilient she has been.

Describe how the other person responded or how the situation shifted: As I was admiring her capacity to endure what's going on at work, I also noticed how determined she was to get this situation resolved. As I consciously held space for what she had to say and consciously listened to what she shared, she suddenly relaxed. I'm not sure why; maybe it was being able to let out all the agony that she'd been holding in. In the middle of her sentence, she stopped and leaned over, and we started hugging each other. When she started to cry, I knew she was releasing the tension in her body.

From your experience, you may notice this is not an easy assignment. You may reflect on how you could have done a better job of holding space and consciously listening to others. That's perfectly normal, especially if you haven't fully shifted your consciousness level to high. No one is there fully, all the time. Sometimes I find myself jumping in to share my point of view without having paid any attention to whether the person I'm with was talking or not. Sometimes I can't stop myself from telling them what to do and how to fix their situation, even when they didn't ask for help. If you find you're still judging, labeling, and so on, that's OK too. The same is true if you're still getting triggered. Try to notice these times and use these experiences as additional opportunities to dive deep into your subconscious internal programming. That is the path. That is your training for life.

The scale of consciousness is fluid and multidimensional. It changes from day to day, mood to mood, energy to energy, situation to situation, and person to person. Just keep in mind that, as you slowly rise to higher consciousness—even though you may fall to lower consciousness from time to time when life asks you to release more sandbags—you will be able to master the act of nondefensive, peaceful, conscious listening with genuine curiosity. And the space you'll be holding will naturally turn into an invitation for others to explore themselves, to release their own sandbags, and to enjoy higher altitudes of consciousness together with you.

ACTIVE SURRENDERING

Another strategy to help you achieve the flow state is called *active surrendering*. It sounds like an oxymoron, right? How can you be active and surrender at the same time?

Active normally implies some kind of activity, movement, or motion. *Surrendering* often indicates passivity. But when you combine the two, your action *is* to take no action. Your decision to do nothing *is actually doing something*—choosing not to act. Active surrendering is, therefore, not about giving in. It's about remaining fully present while going with the flow.

Imagine someone holding your hand and pulling you in one direction to show you something. In active surrendering, you'll make a conscious choice to go along, to see what they're trying to show you. But you remain fully present, and if the situation turns into a threatening one, you know you can always release your hand and turn back.

Through your training so far, you've been building trust in your Self so that you can assertively set healthy boundaries. With this high-conscious strategy, you trust yourself to take charge and adjust boundaries if a situation gets out of control and starts to threaten you. This trust is not available to you when you are in your subconscious realms, between 1 and 55 on that scale of 1 to 100, where your survival mechanisms dominate your life. But now, at these higher levels, you can take more emotional risk. Active surrendering is an inner feeling, an inner reminder to accept and go with the flow of whatever life presents to you without resistance, attachment, defensive action, or the need to control. It's a reminder to face everything in an active, conscious, aware, and assertive state.

Here's another example to illustrate active surrendering. Let's say you call your health insurance provider to get some information about coverage for an upcoming medical test. A robot wants to verify your identity, so you type in your personal data on your phone. You wait fourteen minutes until a live human comes on the line. Now the person needs to verify your identity again. You feel your patience wavering, but you go ahead and provide it. Then, after you ask your question, they say you need to call another department to get your answer. You really start to lose it. But you compose yourself again and call the other number. After another—longer—wait, you go through the same hassle and answer the same questions to verify your identity. After a nine-minute, semifriendly conversation with the new customer service representative, they tell you that you will once again need to talk to someone in another department, and then transfer your call. After a few seconds of silence, you hear a voicemail greeting. You finally lose it!

On other occasions, you may be facing a major challenge in life that feels well beyond your control, such as an abusive partner or the diagnosis of an illness. By no means does active surrendering mean passively accepting what's happening. You don't give in. You don't give up. You consciously process what's going on and listen to your inner feeling about what you can do while maintaining alignment among your mind, body, and heart. You accept what's happening; it is what it is, as they say. But you also stand up for your Self, consciously taking actions within the flow and realm of your higher consciousness.

**Life Skills Assignment #16:
Find a situation that has been a challenge
for you and actively surrender to it.**

This assignment is twofold, and the two parts go hand in hand. One is to practice going with the flow and enjoying the connection to a situation that has been challenging for you in the past. The other is to notice any resistance you feel inside. Let's start by choosing a recent conflict you encountered. Replay it in your mind; you might even want to write down what happened, including the key parts of a tense conversation or something you did that was particularly upsetting. See if you can identify how and when you were able to change the course of events through active surrendering, as well as any inner resistance you felt.

The following is an example of what this assignment might look like.

> *Describe the trigger event:* My boyfriend hasn't texted me back since this morning. He always texts me within a few hours, and now it's late afternoon, and he hasn't responded to my text. I'm going crazy right now. What's going on? Why is he ignoring me? Maybe I was a little too harsh with him last night at dinner when I criticized his idea about getting a juicer.
>
> I said I don't like juicers, as they take all the fiber out of the fruits and vegetables. He said he didn't care. I felt offended that he dismissed my opinion and completely disregarded what I was saying. So, as usual, I criticized him. I said it was a stupid idea and that he wouldn't be juicing anyway, so it'd also be a waste of money. I failed to actively surrender at the moment I became so offended by his dismissal, and now I'm going crazy because he hasn't texted me all day.
>
> *Describe how you used the POWER Method:* And then I remembered to pause. I observed my thoughts about the situation: *He's not texting.* That's the fact. I was able to drop into my body and sense the weight in the pit of my stomach. *What if he's going to leave me?* I acknowledged my fear of abandonment, and my fear of being lonely. I inhaled into my stomach and sat with the weight, and then I simply exhaled it to the earth with the intention of releasing it from my body. After feeling a little

more grounded, I tried to actively surrender to the fact that he hasn't texted yet. What can I do? Then I decided to focus more on what I needed to do that day, instead of obsessing about whether he was going to text me or not. I still noticed some tension in my body, as well as some insecure thoughts lingering in my head, but I didn't check my phone for a while.

Describe how you felt when you actively surrendered: I felt still a little uneasy, yet I was flowing with it. So what if he didn't text me? Maybe something came up or he hadn't seen my texts. Or maybe he *is* losing interest in me or was offended the night before. Even if that were the case, getting grounded and connecting with the earth through the bottoms of my feet helped me stay calmer. For some reason, I accepted all possible outcomes. I was OK with whatever happened.

Describe how the other person responded or how the situation shifted: Within fifteen minutes of when I truly felt calm and grounded, he texted me! "I'm sorry, sweetie, I've been MIA all day. I left my phone at the restaurant last night and have been running around to find a way to get it. Just saw your text. Can't wait to see you tonight."

One of life's biggest dilemmas is the duality that your subconscious creates in your head. It's that mental construct of duality—good versus bad, right versus wrong, success versus failure, beautiful versus ugly, rich versus poor, breakup versus great relationship and so on. At a subconscious level, these two opposite possibilities seem to be the only options you have. This black-and-white approach to life creates a sense of confusion, heaviness, and suffering that affect the quality of your life and make the active surrendering difficult to apply.

Remember though, this polarized outlook belongs in the realms of subconscious survival, where you hide behind your masks and stay in your comfort zone. Going with the flow means moving beyond this frame of mind. Notice that whenever you aren't in the flow, you'll feel stuck and stagnant, which is a state of contraction, where you sense the heaviness of life. Flow, conversely, is a state of expansion where the lightness of life becomes available, as you get closer to Ultimate Happiness.

EFFORTLESS ACTION STATE

After practicing these high-conscious strategies of conscious listening and active surrendering, you'll begin to discover that you're more deeply connecting with your inner feelings, and you'll notice a state of presence that you hadn't felt before. I call this state the *effortless action state*, where you have learned to choose your actions without thinking, strategizing, constructing, or aiming for a goal. Instead, each decision stems from inner knowing, from inner alignment, and it guides you closer to your highest potential without conscious effort.

At this point, you've arrived at a consciousness level where your previous triggers no longer provoke intense emotional reactions. Those old triggers have lost their meaning for you. Consequently, the energy you once spent defending against these old triggers has been freed and restored and is now able to enhance your progress toward living at higher points of integrity—effortlessly.

Law of Life #27:
The higher your consciousness level, the less effort you need to accomplish more.

Here are some examples of how the effortless action state might work for you once you achieve a higher level of consciousness.

> *Partner:* You used to get so angry when your partner was late meeting you. You thought it was their way of dismissing you and devaluing your time. Their tardiness doesn't bother you anymore, and instead of getting annoyed, you appreciate the time to read or listen to music while waiting for them. You love hanging out with your partner over dinner, celebrating your connection and using every available opportunity to learn more about them.

> *Boss:* You used to get triggered when your boss made critical comments regarding your work. Their comments made you feel not good enough, but this is now a moot point for you. You even ask your boss for more feedback, seek clarification, and proactively discuss how you can make your work even better according to their expectations. You are starting to develop a deeper connection with them and better understand where they're coming from.

> *Parents:* You used to get triggered whenever you talked to your parents and found yourself

in conflict. You always left their house tense
and irritated, certain the interaction had
ruined your entire day. Now you can stand up
for your boundaries. Without guilt, you have
started to say no. You no longer do things
that aren't aligned with your values simply
to please them, and you're able to have pleasant chats and meaningful conversations with
them. The doors for deeper connections have
opened, revealing childhood memories that
demonstrate how much they love you.

Parents-in-law: You used to dread going to your
parents-in-law's house. They always talked
about subjects that intimidated you, or they
made comments that made you feel not good
enough, or they pressured you about having
children. Now you have come to accept them
for who they are, and your defensive energies
have been replaced by curiosity. Instead of getting nervous, you carry a sense of wonder with
you, and you've found that they are better able
to connect with your new authentic Self than
with your old anxious one. It's definitely been
a great start for the future of your relationship
with them.

Traffic: You used to get triggered when a driver
cut you off on the highway. Nowadays, traffic
may not bother you as much, as you understand that some drivers need to rush because
they're running late to their appointments. You
pay more attention to your audiobook while
driving. You arrive at your morning meetings

with more energy, and as a result, you come up with more creative ideas for your team. You have more productive days at work, and when you return home, you embrace your partner with more love. You even occasionally surprise them with a gift you spontaneously picked up on your way home: chocolate mousse! You enjoy dinner and are more attentive to your kids before bedtime.

You may find yourself in even more challenging situations that have triggered you in the past: unemployment, illness, abuse, infidelity, discrimination, trauma, and so forth. At one time you may have thought it impossible to experience the state of effortless action in the face of these troubles, but the same practices and principles still apply. You still practice the POWER Method. You still integrate your polarities. You stand up by doing the opposite. You set healthy boundaries with I-statements. You follow your heart values. You learn the beauty of conscious listening and active surrendering. And you'll be amazed at what might arise once you've achieved the effortless action state.

Maybe as you sit with the discomfort of unemployment with your eyes closed, listening to your inner knowing, a name from the past will pop into your mind. You'll send them a quick text to reconnect and find that it leads you to an employment opportunity. Maybe you'll have more energy to research alternative treatment options for your disease. Or maybe you'll now be able to acknowledge your resistance but maintain a state of active surrendering upon receiving the devastating news of your partner's infidelity.

The POWER Method and the integration process have prepared you to face and embrace all life, the good and the bad. The invitation in effortless action is to understand that, in addition to external resources, you have internal tools that promote higher alignment between your mind, heart, and body.

Life Skills Assignment #17:
Practice an effortless action state by taking
conscious actions to achieve flow.

While facing a challenging situation, practice the effortless action state and take conscious actions to flow with what's happening. Write down the difficulties you had aligning your mind, heart, and body with each other. Note the consequences and openings that resulted from the integration. If you can't achieve full alignment and feel out of the flow, simply observe what it feels like without self-judgment.

Now write down some actions in your daily review journal that you can take to help you with your integration process, to improve your alignment, and to achieve a state of flow.

Here's an example of what this could look like:

> *Describe the trigger event:* Another late night. I'm completely exhausted. My eyes are burning. My body is tired. Yet I'm still on my phone, scrolling the social feeds of my friends, switching back and forth among Facebook, Instagram, and Twitter. I'm completely out of the flow now. I'm annoyed at myself that I can't pull away from my phone and stop looking at social media. I want to go to bed. I want to rest. My body feels heavy from tiredness. Yet I feel a subtle force that I can't resist; it pulls me back into this pleasurable activity of scrolling down

the newsfeed of my friends, looking at their vacation pictures, imagining myself being there one day, checking out how they decorated their houses, googling the restaurants they went to, and so on.

Describe how you used the POWER Method: While experiencing irritation, and some joy, from all of this, I remember to pause, take a step back, and immediately observe that I also feel some jealousy and resentment toward these friends. As my emotions puzzle me, I drop into my body and further observe the tension around my neck, heaviness on my shoulders, and tightness in my fingers, the way I grip my phone, and the exhaustion all through my body. I'm completely out of alignment, out of the flow. After dropping into my body, I remember the three-by-three breath work to welcome the physical sensations. I take a deep breath into my tense neck and hold it for three seconds. Sitting with that pain in my neck makes me realize how desperate I am for connection and social interaction. I exhale to the earth, imagining the tension leaving my body, going out of my feet and into the floor. I do this two more times.

Describe how you aligned your mind, heart, and body and prepared yourself for effortless action: I now feel some relief and have created space that helps me observe my Self more attentively as I scroll through the social media news feeds. I now become curious. What am I doing here? What do I want to get out of this thing? Why do I get pulled into social media? I feel the heaviness of fatigue even more; it's getting harder to keep my eyes open. I can't believe I am being reeled back into the limiting life pattern that has happened every night for the last two or three years.

I start to feel the tension building up again. I go for a second round of three-by-three breath work. After the third exhale to earth the tension off my body, I finally observe some emptiness within me. Slowly I notice the fear of loneliness creeping up. I feel chills. My body starts to shake a little bit with deep apprehension of being lonely, with no one to talk to, no one to share my memories with, no one to be with for the rest of my life.

Depression and loneliness begin to overwhelm me, but I stay with them. I pause, step back again, and observe the thoughts trying to pull me back to my phone. But I also notice my heart wanting to go to bed and my body completely torn between the two. Now, as I observe all of them together, I feel calm and relaxed. I turn my attention one more time to my feet to connect with the earth, and I remain grounded and observant of the different pulls within my Self.

Describe your effortless action: I go back to social media and simply watch my Self, as if I am an objective observer, as my news feed scrolls. I acknowledge my joy when I "like" a post. I also consciously notice my jealousy when looking at

one of my friend's vacation pictures in Hawai'i.
And, of course, I "like" that post too. This *going-
with-the-flow* attitude makes me conscious of
exactly what I am doing, moment by moment,
and why I'm doing it.

*Describe how you felt after practicing effortless
action:* All of a sudden, I find myself naturally
relaxing. As the calmness slowly settles within
my body, my mind connects with my heart,
and my body effortlessly puts the phone down.
I close my eyes, staying there for a few more
minutes. When it feels right, I get up and go to
bed. After I wake up the next morning, I realize I slept better than I had in a long time.

When you get back in a flow state like in the above experience, when a trigger flies by without affecting you emotionally, and you can stand there without getting pulled into your
old ways, into your old destructive habits, you get a sense of
an energetic shift into a higher level of consciousness, where
effortless action is more available, more possible to do. Imagine
life is a river streaming toward you, bringing all sorts of opportunities and possibilities. Even though they may be challenging and difficult to face, these opportunities and possibilities
invite you to go inward. What if you just stand there, embracing and accepting what comes to you with open eyes, with full
awareness?

When you respond to the stream of life coming to you,
you basically deal with whatever is in front of you, in that very
moment. You just wait to act until the right time, not a second too soon, not a second too late. And when you move, you
choose your actions according to your own values, all aligned
with the mental, emotional, and physical layers of your Self,

instead of the values that others impose on you or expect you to live by. You are getting ready to have your authentic flow to claim your own unique place and presence in the world.

LIVING FROM A PLACE OF
HIGH INTEGRITY

By now, most of your sandbags have been released from your hot air balloon, allowing you to experience the smooth sailing of higher altitudes. "What's next?"

Well, let's go back to our story about the two monks traveling on a muddy road. Tanzan and Ekido had conflicting views about how to properly deal with a young woman in need of help. What do you think is the biggest differentiating factor between Tanzan, who followed his own value system, and Ekido, who was stuck in dogmatic rules?

Presence!

Tanzan had an unyielding presence. He wasn't bothered by outside influences or judgments; he didn't change his behavior to accommodate expectations or critical observations. How can you create such presence? Through reclaiming your essence—the inner spirit of who you really are.

You have been bringing down the walls of your conditioned self, the layers of your protective mask, the pulls of your hidden desires, the chains of your cultural to-dos, the obligations of societal norms, the expectations of others, your parental conditioning, and the heaviness of social and environmental pressures since the first day you stepped onto this path. Now let me introduce you to someone who's been waiting for you at the end of the road: your Real Self.

Who is your Real Self?

The one whose sandbags are released, whose repressed fears are processed. The one whose mask is removed and whose hidden desires are integrated. The one who is self-aware and lives consciously, high above subconscious internal programming. The one who lives in perfect flow, at peace, grounded and centered in the present. The one who has achieved a sense of individual freedom and emotional mastery—and who has experienced glimpses of Ultimate Happiness and what it means to fully embrace life with joy, fulfillment, and purpose.

Like Tanzan, your Real Self is a solid, strong individual traveler of life, well connected within the inner self as well as with others outside. Your Real Self lives from a place of high integrity, which I define as complete integration of mind, heart, and body.

What does this presence, this high integrity state, look like in life?

Let's say you don't like your job. Before you started your journey of self-discovery, your mind might have said, *I hate my job!* and your heart might have responded with a suggestion to take time off and go on a vacation. Meanwhile, your body might have been confounded about where to go or what to do. *I'm just going to go out with some friends tonight, get drunk, and forget about everything.*

This might have been a typical situation under the influence of your subconscious internal programming, with your mind, heart, and body wishing for and pushing different agendas. At the self-conscious level, you might have still hated your job, but you learned to pivot your reaction to response. You asked *why?* and *what if?* instead. You practiced doing the opposite, I-statements, and honoring your heart values.

Now you've reached a high-conscious level, and this is where you find high integrity—integration of mind, heart, and body—utilizing the self-knowledge you've gained along this journey. At this point of high integrity, you are now able to reflect on your internal conflicts and listen to your inner feelings and inner knowing. You can see different options appear in front of you that flow with the situation you are in. For example, you may decide to talk to your boss about how you can get more fulfillment from your job, or discuss the possibility of getting transferred to another department, or call recruiters to find another job, or try to switch from a manager position to an individual contributor or vice versa. When you stand back and consciously receive the stream of life flowing toward you, opportunities appear in front of you. You no longer see things in black and white. In other words, you can now connect with many different options at this higher consciousness level than are available at a lower level.

CONNECTING WITH INNER
FEELINGS OF HIGH INTEGRITY

Integration isn't all-or-nothing. Your mind, heart, and body can align in some aspects of your life but remain misaligned in others. Becoming integrated also isn't a linear process. You can rise up, but you may fall back down, and then you get up and give it another go, maybe trying a different strategy or shifting your reaction the next time you face another trigger. What's constant in this whole process is that you become increasingly aware of your inner feelings, which in turn makes it easier and easier to achieve a place of high integrity and remain there.

The following is a list of those inner feelings you may experience when you reach that point of high integrity and stay present at higher consciousness levels.

Compassion

Deep understanding of someone's fears and desires and why they do things the way they do. This inner knowing opens the way to spreading love and compassion around you and throughout your community. Compassion naturally arises within you when you truly understand your Self and realize higher consciousness levels. Compassion is the opposite of hate, anger, resentment, and rage. When you gain a deeper understanding of others and their suffering, you will begin to drop your labels, judgments, and perceptions. But without first knowing your Self, it's difficult to know and understand somebody else. Try not to force it as a mental construct, such as *I should be more compassionate now*, when you're angry. As you ascend to higher consciousness levels, compassion will rise with you. Be patient.

Gratitude

Joyful acknowledgement of the impact and influence that people, things, and situations have on your personal, professional, and spiritual life. Gratitude is the opposite of regret. Whereas regret is the wish that you could change the past, gratitude brings you to the present. The high-conscious level of gratitude can be achieved only when everything in your past makes sense. Try not to force it mentally; gratitude will show up when you are well settled at high-conscious levels.

Forgiveness

Release of others from their responsibility to act in a certain way according to your expectations, beliefs, or value system. Forgiveness acknowledges your pain but accepts the wrongdoing of others. This acceptance is the opposite of judgment, and it's not available until you reach higher consciousness levels. Through understanding your own nature and conditioning, you will become able to forgive. Until then, sit with whatever comes up.

Joy and Inspiration

Feelings of flow. Connection with deeper creativity. You may feel joy out of nowhere as a sentiment toward life, whereas its cousin, inspiration, derives from the desire to fully experience life through your own self-expression. Guilt is the opposite of joy and inspiration. When you rise to higher consciousness levels, and you connect more intimately with your Self, you discover self-acceptance and self-love, and access to a deeper creativity that flows through you, which together drive you to embrace life to its fullest. You naturally release guilt from your system and live life in the flow according to your true nature and essence.

Inner Knowing

The sixth sense. Your intuition. Inner knowing manifests as what we call a gut feeling. The opposite of inner knowing is survival. Once you rise to high-conscious levels, this inner knowing permeates your daily decisions more and more. You act intuitively. You follow your gut more. You find your flow. In a sense, inner knowing is preparation for your highest integrity point, where your mind, heart, and body are fully aligned and waiting for you to climb one more step to reach your Ultimate Happiness.

Grace and Presence

The ability to effortlessly and actively participate in the flow of life. Grace is the elegant zone state, where you flow in your own lane, according to your own values, without being impacted by the chaos happening around you. All other inner feelings come together to support you. Along with grace comes presence, which is the feeling of being complete, fully integrated. Shame is the opposite of grace and presence. When you have arrived at your highest consciousness level, you have also found your Real Self and achieved your highest potential, your highest integrity point. Here you experience a life of joy, love, abundance, fulfillment, and meaning. Here is where you find Ultimate Happiness.

Life Skills Assignment #18:
Tune in and notice whenever you glimpse inner feelings of high integrity and note how they affect your connections and interactions with others and with the world at large.

Inner feelings and high integrity aren't things you can force or make yourself do, so trying to complete an assignment along these lines might feel stilted and synthetic. One of the best ways I've found for practicing abstract concepts is making a pact with my Self for a period of time, say a week, to just notice and record in my journal.

For this assignment, for example, you might promise yourself to describe in your journal at the end of each day, for just one week, every time you notice one particular feeling of integrity, such as compassion. Maybe you'll sense a warm feeling in your chest that arises from deep understanding of someone whose conditioned self you intimately know, because it was you before, when you see one of your colleagues jumping into every conversation, trying so hard to be recognized at one of your boss's weekly meetings. Maybe, on another occasion, you notice how your partner takes charge of so many things around the house with the pure intention of taking care of you and the kids, without asking much other than your love and appreciation, and you feel the pull to give them a big, warm, intimate hug to show your appreciation and love.

These and many other moments of high integrity are waiting for you. Just pay attention to those moments and make a note of your inner feelings as they bubble up. Then simply follow their energy by taking spontaneous actions, effortlessly flowing with whatever is arising.

Here's an example of what this assignment may look like.

Describe your high integrity feeling: Forgiveness.

Describe when you felt your high integrity feeling and how you applied the energy of that inner feeling to the situation at hand: I was talking to my dad the other day. I felt frustrated at the way he was ignoring my thoughts and instead wanted to talk about stuff that was important to him. Not being acknowledged by him, or even not being seen by him, has been the main issue in my life that affected many of my relationships. As soon as I felt the frustration, I applied the POWER Method, and I noticed an immediate centeredness. This feeling of being grounded has not been available to me for a long time when in his presence, as the emotional hurt of not being seen by him runs very deep. But after working on it for the last couple of years, I was finally able to step back from our interaction, and I realized something shocking. *My dad wants to be seen by me.* Where did that realization come from? I then noticed, once I stepped out of my own hidden desire to be seen and recognized, a profoundly natural feeling of forgiveness.

Describe how the others responded to your high integrity feeling. When I shifted away from my hidden desire to talk about myself in an attempt to be seen, and I stripped off the mask of my conditioned self, I was able to consciously listen to my dad talk about himself. As I held space for my dad to express himself, he started sharing stories from his younger days, which he'd usually avoided in the past. To my surprise, he also asked me a few small questions about my personal life. Finally, we were having the kind of flow in our conversation that I'd been craving for decades.

At the end of the week, review what you noticed and wrote down each day. Do you see some patterns developing? Does anything surprise you? Sometimes the more we notice, the more effortlessly we're able to shift; this assignment is meant to help you do just that.

CHAPTER NINE

EMBRACING THE NEW LIFE, THE NEW YOU

We are about to conclude our journey together and say our farewells. Before you leave to explore your New Life on your own and experience your New You, at your highest potential and with Ultimate Happiness, I'd like to share something that has been fascinating me since the first day I left the corporate world: the matrix.

Have you watched the movie *The Matrix*?

Over the years, my clients have told me about this movie, mentioning some scenes from it they thought had some unbelievable parallels to the work they had done with me. The first time I watched the movie, I didn't understand a thing. I thought it was a violent sci-fi movie, and I didn't think too much of it. Over time I forgot all about it, but when my clients repeatedly mentioned the relevant scenes, I had no choice but to watch it again.

When I did, I was shocked! I couldn't believe how tightly the core message of *The Matrix* fit to the transformation journey in my Rise 2 Realize POWER Method. I've never met the producers, writers, or directors, and certainly in 1999, when the movie was released—and when I was thirty-two years of age—I didn't have any clue about how the System of Life worked or what on earth a transformation journey meant. I had to go through my own transformation and shift my consciousness to understand what was meant in *The Matrix*.

If you haven't watched the movie before, I highly recommend it. Of course, I've watched it a few more times, since my clients never stopped making references to it. In my opinion, *The Matrix* is a captivating presentation of a consciousness shift and a well-illustrated hero's journey of personal transformation. It's the most brilliantly reflected and storied journey on the silver screen.

A computer scientist named Thomas Anderson is invited by Morpheus to see the reality that humanity has been trapped within, a computer-simulated life created by machines that use human bodies as an energy source. Thomas agrees to "take the red pill" and join forces with Morpheus, who renames him Neo and takes him under his wing so that, together, they can save the world. Morpheus believes Neo is "the one" who will lead the human liberation movement to freedom from the slavery of the machines.

Guess who Neo is? It's YOU! Neo is, of course, You!

You are the chosen one who faces the energy-draining machines: those demons of ego that make you react and that deplete you, leaving you exhausted over and over again. You are also the one who takes the red pill, signifying your decision to break free from the captivity of your subconscious internal programming, which is essentially your matrix—the force that keeps you stuck in the cycle of your limiting life patterns and all the suffering that comes with it. You are the one on the journey of individual freedom and emotional mastery to rise above what controls and holds you back, to realize Ultimate

Happiness and its unbounded state of joy, love, abundance, fulfillment, and meaning. You are the one who becomes renewed
and lives as the beacon of authenticity, according to your true
nature and essence, acting from high integrity.

How did you become Neo?

Just for fun, let's review how your journey of transformation toward higher consciousness is reflected in three major
scenes in *The Matrix*. (Spoiler alert!)

The first major scene: Subconscious level: 1 through 55.
Morpheus is training Neo in kung fu fighting in a martial arts
studio. After a few punches, Morpheus sees Neo struggle.

"Don't *think* about hitting me," he says. "Just hit me."

His invitation is obviously to drop from the mind into the
body. Neo was still living according to his subconscious internal programming, and his mind was getting in the way of his
full integration. He needed to get out of his head and connect
with his body to start the integration process.

And that's exactly what you did in the beginning of your
journey. The practice of self-observation was all about noticing your thoughts and the physical sensations in your body, so
you could create some space between you and your thoughts
and thus drop into the body when you connected your thumbs.
And whenever you were triggered and found yourself in a limiting life pattern cycle, you learned to PAUSE and OBSERVE
your thoughts, no matter how busy your mind was. Once
you dropped into your body and anchored your focus on the
physical sensation of your thumbs, you became an objective
observer of your Self. You also began to experience tiny little
glimpses of your presence.

The second major scene: Self-conscious level: 56 through
85. This is the most famous scene of *The Matrix*. Neo is on top
of a building and facing the machines, who want to kill him

because he's becoming more and more of a threat to them. It's a face-off. The machines fire their guns, and we're sure Neo is going to get killed. (But it's only the middle of the movie, and he's our hero, so we know that can't happen.) The machines are powerful and relentless, like our limiting life patterns. There seems to be no escape from them, but then, thanks to his training with Morpheus, Neo has learned to slow everything down so much that he's now faster than bullets. He can literally dodge them as they travel through the air toward him.

This is exactly how you feel when you experience your first moment of dodging a trigger and everything around you slows down. Things, thoughts, conversations start to happen in slow motion. Once you get into that objective-observer state, you create the time and space to consciously respond to triggers the way you want.

Since Neo is no longer living his life according to the will of the machines, he can deal with his discomfort. Likewise, you no longer need to adhere to the rules of your subconscious internal programming, so you can WELCOME your discomfort and suffering more easily. As he drops into his body, Neo learns to sit with the sensations of his repressed fears and gains new flexibility, agility, and vitality in his body. He is slowly leaving the matrix—the structure that bound his soul. As in this scene, you will notice in real life that, after facing a trigger, you will recover much more quickly. The impact of the trigger will also be less emotionally draining than before you started your journey. Once you experience this shift as an inner feeling, your life is never going to be the same. Welcome to your self-conscious level.

The third major scene: High-conscious level: 86 through 100. Neo, having been chased by the machines throughout the movie, finally gets caught in the narrow hallway of an old building. He is killed, and you think humans now don't stand a chance of breaking free from the Matrix. You also wonder how Neo could die. *Wasn't he the chosen one?* You are devastated; after all, you cheered for him throughout the movie, as if it were you who was fighting against the machines for your own individual freedom.

Well, wait! *Neo* means *new*, and sure enough, Neo starts to move his body, slowly and painfully getting up. You know he's hurting, but now he stands a little taller and shakes himself off, like dusting off sandbags. He returns to the hallway to yet again face off against the machines—his demons, his dragons. And now you can see he doesn't have any fear in his eyes anymore. You can tell, with his death—the death of his ego—he discharged all of his repressed fears and hidden desires off to earth. What's standing up is his new Self, his true nature, his essence.

Grounded and centered, he invites the machines to fire their bullets. And oh boy, they do! Hundreds of bullets fill the air, heading toward Neo. What does our hero do? Neo slowly raises his hand and stops the bullets right before they cross his personal boundaries. He PAUSES everything. He carefully OBSERVES the bullets hanging in the air, right in front of him. He WELCOMES one of the bullets by taking it in his hand and gazing at it with curiosity. He can't figure out what a bullet means anymore. Triggers lose their meaning when you don't have any repressed fears that feed your perceptions. Fully present, he lets the bullet drop, and all the remaining bullets fall to the EARTH. Neo then RISES above the threat and destroys the machines, and as he flies to higher altitudes, he promises a world without machines and an end to human captivity.

I wish your personal transformation could take place in two hours, sixteen minutes, and nineteen seconds, as Neo's did in the movie. On the other hand, maybe, in real life, you will find your New You in just two years, sixteen weeks, and nineteen days. I hope you do. Who knows? But as long as you're committed to your training, to your journey, you will certainly release your sandbags completely and free your Self from the confines of your subconscious internal programming.

My journey started fourteen years and four months ago, and you pretty much learned what has happened since then as you've read through the pages of this guidebook. Today, I wouldn't say of myself that I am constantly living at a high-conscious level—because life happens. But I do think I'm living about 55 percent of my life in that joyful, loving, abundant, ful-filled, and meaningful state that I've come to know as Ultimate Happiness.

My recovery rate from a trigger is on average within an hour, depending on the severity. For example, there was one major trigger a few months ago that took two days to shake off, meaning it kept coming back to my mind, and I kept getting hooked by the old, recurring story in my head: my past per-ceived reality of not being recognized, not being understood, not being seen. It happens. It took a while to go all the way down to the bottom of the sandbags that held these repressed fears, and to slowly and gently integrate them back into my Real Self.

My responses to triggers are far more than just emotional reactions nowadays. My curiosity about life continues to grow, along with my ability to enjoy personal freedom of expression. Again, I'm not fully there yet, because this journey of self-discovery and eventual self-realization is an up-and-down, back-and-forth one. It's also multidimensional. I can master one area of my life, and then I might fall down a few steps in another area. I climb back up, just to discover another area needing some attention for personal and spiritual growth.

Eventually it all comes together, and I feel in the flow again, even invincible, for a few days or weeks. Then another trigger hits me. I know, when that happens, life is just humbling me again. It's reminding me to return to my study of Self. And when I do, I acquire further, deeper self-knowledge with every experience that I embrace. I see new glimpses of how everything, and everyone, is connected. With my renewed, deep understanding, I keep walking until walking becomes just walking, without effort.

How will you know that you're well on your path toward Ultimate Happiness?

Well, do you remember the state of your being in the beginning of your journey, before we even started exploring the POWER Method? Do you remember how a trigger affected you? Do you remember the intensity of your anger, frustration, sadness, and hurt? How long did it take, back then, to shake off the negative consequences of an offensive comment or nasty attitude? Was it days? Weeks?

Now notice what has happened along the way since then. How do you react when you're triggered now? Is it as intense as before? Do you fall as low as before? Does the negative emotional impact on your mental state linger as long as before?

One of the best indicators that you are walking on the right path toward your highest potential, your Ultimate Happiness, is that you don't react as intensely as before. Another is that you don't fall as low as before. And a third indicator is that the impact of the triggers doesn't last as long as it once did.

Law of Life #28:
Life meets you exactly where you are.
Your consciousness level determines
what kind of life you experience.

Do you remember our hot air balloon analogy? When you rise to higher altitudes, you access different experiences at each level of consciousness. Surprisingly, and wondrously, life will also meet you exactly at your level, presenting various people and situations based on your altitude. If you keep blaming life and people for challenges and wrongdoings, life will bring you more sets of challenging scenarios. In those moments, if you turn your attention inward to work on your own sandbags and eventually process them fully, you'll notice that you have a completely different, more grandiose, more rewarding, more vibrant set of life experiences with completely different opportunities and possibilities.

Below are some life scenarios that demonstrate the application of this incredible phenomenon, the System of Life.

Love Life

When two people meet, they usually share a consciousness level. Let's say a couple meets at consciousness level 22. One of them does some personal growth work and, after rising to level 32 in a few months, begins to express their needs with I-statements. How would their partner respond to this?

One alternative is that their partner would listen, and together they'd start communicating more openly about each other's needs. They'd develop a new flow or alchemy in the fresh structure of this relationship, and together they might both rise to even higher levels, where conflicts become rarer and less intense. The other possibility is that their partner ignores their needs, disregards their vulnerability, and chooses to stay stuck at 22 or so. In that case, this couple will experience a lot of conflicts, soul searching, frustrations, and blame as their consciousness level together now hovers around 27. This doesn't mean that they need to break up; it merely provides an invitation for them to work closely together to heighten their awareness and deepen their intimacy.

Career Choices

The same situation applies to careers. When you choose your career right out of college, you are mostly subject to your mind values, so let's say your consciousness level is 15. At that level, your decisions are mainly based on your survival mechanisms, such as what others expect from you and what your financial needs might be. If you stay in that field and maintain a similar survival mode of operation, later in your career, you may run into challenges like loss of motivation, conflicts with coworkers, and difficult bosses.

In that case, one alternative would be to express your needs to yourself and reassess your values. Find out what's important to you and follow up with conscious actions to honor those values that are missing in your life. Without resigning or completely shifting your career, you can still increase your consciousness level by acting on those values. You might, for example, honor your creative interests and spend your weekends going to nature reserves to take some pictures. This in turn will give you more energy at work. Can you imagine how your life will be different then? Where will your consciousness be? Let's say you rise to level 42.

Alternatively, you might not make any changes. You simply don't take any actions or clarify your heart or mind values. You keep complaining about your job and remain stuck and unhappy. Your comfort zone contracts, and your consciousness level drops. How do you think life is going to be moving forward? At that level, it is going to be tough. You might experience anger—and not just at work, but at home as well. You might find yourself frustrated with small things. You might lose your cool when things don't go the way you want them to go because you're in a place you don't want to be and you don't know how to get out.

Family Life

The same principles also apply to raising kids. When you become a parent, your survival instincts get heightened. Now you have someone you need to take care of and look after. What if something bad happens to this innocent, defenseless, sweet baby? Lower consciousness levels are naturally subject to more intense subconscious internal programming, which means higher fear-based content. As a parent operating at a lower level, your actions and choices will naturally be fear-based. If you start out at level 19 with your newborn, where might you go from there? Where would your kids go?

The more fear-based your parenting style, the more reactive your kids will be. They'll have more tantrums than peers raised in less fear-based households. They'll suffer from more separation anxieties, or have trouble interacting with others, or struggle with academic performance and self-confidence. For a parent who remains at level 19, this would be the typical flow of their life.

Alternatively, you can change this trajectory by taking a step back and looking at your own Self and values. In that process, you might discover you need to deal with your own fears before starting a family. Or if you already have kids, maybe you'll decide to be more open with them and explain to them where you're coming from by using I-statements, or enter into dialogues in which you honestly discuss why you make the choices you make. Maybe through your work, you'll focus on finding balance between discipline and a relaxed upbringing. This alternative approach will allow your children to intuitively know your mental and emotional state and to feel your presence. They'll understand how you want to communicate and maybe how you feel inside. If you're open to shifting your level, you might rise higher than you'd expect and begin to experience a flow with your child. If you experience them with less fear in your heart, hold space for them, consciously listen to them, and be present for them, you may very well witness a consciousness shift for both you and your kids, rising to levels of 45 and above.

Dating Scene

Of course, dating is no exception when it comes to levels of consciousness. When you're on the dating scene, it is easy to wonder where those great people are, the ideal candidates who will bring you the happiness you have been looking for. Of course, they are nowhere to be found. One disappointment after another, you keep running into subpar candidates for love, and you lose faith in dating. What's happening here? What's your consciousness level? Are you too dependent on someone else for happiness? What's your purpose in dating? Is it fear-based? Is it desperation?

Without having done this work, let's say your level is 28. At this level, you will attract potential mates who are more or less at level 28. You might not like those you meet because in your heart, you know you can do better than 28. Even though you might be disappointed and frustrated, without working on your Self, you continue making the same choices, your consciousness remains at the same level, and you keep meeting similar people.

A different path might be to take some time to learn about your repressed fears and hidden desires. Maybe you can also learn to approach your dates with curiosity instead of trying to check off attributes you think your mate should have. When you shift your approach and take some conscious actions like these, you will rise to, let's say, level 41. And soon you'll notice a change in the dates you go on. There will be greater emotional intimacy, mental connection, and physical chemistry between you. At this new level of consciousness, you'll keep learning more about your Self and also enjoy the profound flow with this person you just met. Together you can explore the more intimate, more honest, and more sincere interactions of this mutually rewarding dating relationship at a higher consciousness level.

Friend Circles

What happens to your circle of friends when you rise in your consciousness levels? Friendships are formed due to commonalities: interests, backgrounds, emotional needs, goals, intentions, and so on. When you meet a friend at a consciousness level of 26, and that's where you are too, everything's great. But you may have already noticed that things are changing between you now that you've been on this journey for a while. And just as you're adjusting to the changes, your friends are as well.

Let's say you've moved up to 40 but your friends haven't. Now you have a different flow in life, and you might not relate as well to each other. One possible consequence of this situation could be that you start to feel lonely and contract into your comfort zone—and your old ways—to keep your friends. To avoid that, you could open up your curiosity and express it to them. Some of them might even want to share your journey and join you on the path to Ultimate Happiness. Alternatively, your higher level might lead you to pursue new intellectual, creative, or artistic interests, and you might make new friendships.

At any given moment, you have the power to choose, and whatever you choose will be according to your consciousness level. What's important is not which level you're on, but that you *own* your level. If you don't like how life greets you, take a step back and notice your consciousness level. Recall that your sandbags are keeping you at that level. Use the POWER Method to release them and rise to the next level, to open a new set of doors, and to greet opportunities to live a life according to your Real Self.

Law of Life #29:
Integrated self is the Real Self
who creates presence.

Have you heard the story "The Samurai and the Tea Master?"[1] It takes place several centuries ago in Japan. A tea master worked in the service of Lord Yamanouchi. He conducted his tea ceremonies so perfectly that no one came close to his skill and precision. The timing and grace of his every move, from the unfurling of the mat, to the setting out of the cups, to the sifting of the green leaves, was pure elegance, beauty, and divinity. Lord Yamanouchi was so pleased with his tea master that he bestowed upon him the rank and robes of a samurai warrior.

When Lord Yamanouchi traveled, he always took his tea master with him, so that others could appreciate the perfection of his art. On one occasion, they went on business to the great city of Edo, which is now known as Tokyo. When evening fell, the tea master and his friends set out to explore the city. But as they turned a corner, they found themselves face-to-face with two samurai warriors.

The tea master bowed and politely stepped into the gutter to let the fearsome duo pass. Although one samurai went by, the other remained rooted to the spot. He stroked a long black whisker that decorated his face, which had been gnarled by the sun and scarred by the sword. His eyes pierced the tea master's heart like an arrow.

The samurai did not quite know what to make of this fellow who also dressed like a warrior, yet would willingly step aside into a gutter, so cowardly, so shamefully. He looked the tea master up and down and started to think he was an imposter, a loser, just pretending to be a noble samurai. He finally stamped the ground like a raging bull and exclaimed, "He who wears the robes of a samurai must fight like a samurai. I challenge you to a duel. If you die with dignity, you will bring honor to your ancestors. And if you die like a dog, at least you will no longer insult the rank of the samurai!" He stated the time and the place for the mortal contest.

Completely terrified and trembling about this incredible challenge, the tea master ran back to Lord Yamanouchi and told him the entire story.

"Master, I have one day and one night to learn how to die with honor. Can you teach me how to die like a samurai?"

Lord Yamanouchi had great respect for the master of the tea ceremony. "I will teach you all you require, but first, I ask that you perform the Way of the Tea for me one last time."

The tea master could not refuse this request. As he performed the ceremony, all trace of fear seemed to leave his face. He was serenely concentrated on the simple but beautiful cups and pots, and the delicate aroma of the leaves. There was no room in his mind for anxiety. His thoughts were focused on the ritual.

When the ceremony was complete, his master slapped his thigh and exclaimed with pleasure, "There you have it. No need to learn anything of the way of death. Your state of mind when you perform the tea ceremony is all that is required. When you see your challenger tomorrow, imagine that you are about to serve tea for him. Salute him courteously, express regret that you could not meet him sooner, take off your coat, and fold it as you did just now. Wrap your head in a silken scarf and do it with the same serenity as you dress for the tea ritual. Draw your sword and hold it high above your head. Then close your eyes and ready yourself for combat."

That is exactly what the tea master did when, at the crack of dawn the following morning, he met his opponent. The samurai warrior had been expecting a quivering wreck, and he was amazed by the tea master's presence of mind as he prepared himself for combat. The samurai's eyes were now opened; he saw a different man altogether. The warrior bowed, asked to be excused for his rude behavior, and left the place of combat with as much dignity as he could muster.

You create your presence with your Real Self, not from a borrowed societal norm, or from an acceptable image in a community, or from wearing masks to meet others' approval. Your journey has been a path of self-discovery that led you to individual freedom and emotional mastery. The invitation for the rest of your life is to create that presence to access your highest potential—your Ultimate Happiness. Your presence is founded on a set of inner values that make you who you are and that's connected to your own principles and vision of life. It's built according to your own true nature and essence, unbounded by any societal norms or expectations of others.

This presence is already within you. It's within your own body, quietly awaiting discovery through those nudges from your limiting life patterns that we explored earlier. This is by design, courtesy of life's calling for your personal and spiritual growth toward higher consciousness.

Life Skills Assignment #19:
Fully embrace your New Life, your New
You, and stay in harmonious flow with
your essence and true nature.

As with many new ways of living, we must practice in order to ingrain new habits, perspectives, and approaches to life. Learning to embrace your New You and live harmoniously in your New Life is no different. Using all of the skills you've learned throughout these pages, as well as your daily review journal, you are ready to practice this final assignment.

Here's an example of what it might look like, with some question prompts to help you.

Describe how you felt when you were out of the flow: I was in Turkey, visiting my family over Christmas break. I was excited to be back and to see my family and friends, which used to be a painful experience before my self-discovery journey, because old hurts always resurfaced from my childhood and high school years. This year, it was different. Having done some work on my repressed fears and old wounds, I was relaxed and looking forward to connecting with everyone. I was feeling good and in the flow.

One day, I decided to visit a friend. My mom asked me how I was planning to get there. I said I was going to walk. She was shocked that I was going to walk for an hour to visit my friend, rather than take a cab to get there in ten minutes. I said I needed to move my body after a long flight home. She insisted that it wasn't a good idea. She suggested alternatives, like having my sister drop me off or meeting my friend closer to us. I abruptly lost it. I felt my judgment was questioned; I felt pressured to do something that she wanted; I felt suffocated by all her insistence. I felt controlled, exactly the way I'd felt while growing up.

Describe how you used the POWER Method and integration process to release your sandbags, rise to a high-conscious level, and find your flow again: This was a tough one. The feeling of being controlled had been such a deep wound that I couldn't apply POWER immediately. But when I managed to pause, I noticed my frustration. I observed my thoughts in my head: *I feel controlled. I have lost my freedom.* Next, I dropped into my body and connected with the physical sensation in the center of my chest. It was a heavy force clamping down. I immediately ran the integration process. First, I moved that heavy feeling from my chest to my right hand, made a fist, and called it *caged.* Then, I called the opposite feeling *free*, felt it in my throat, moved it to my left hand, and made a fist. After integrating my repressed fears of being *caged* and my hidden desires to be *free*, I felt neutral, grounded, and centered, and not bound by my mom's comments. I wasn't getting hooked into my usual limiting life pattern cycle. I was back in the flow again.

Describe how you felt when you got back into the flow: I felt an inner sense of freedom. I saw that my mom simply wanted me to be safe, happy, and well-rested after a long plane flight. I acknowledged and accepted that she didn't understand why I wanted to walk. It was OK that she didn't get me. I was no longer triggered. At the same time, I didn't need to change my plans to please her. I stayed present and firm with my intention to walk so that I could revitalize my body with some movement.

As a result, right there and then, I had a new revelation: although my mom wanted to control my actions, I'd always had the power to make my own choices. In my youth, I *thought* I needed to exchange my freedom for food, love, and shelter, but this was a perceived reality; my parents' love for me was never conditional on whether I obeyed them. I had spent all those years not knowing I'd had that freedom to choose in my hands all along. The truth of the matter is I wasn't at a higher consciousness level to claim that individual freedom. I didn't have the power to go against the force of my people-pleaser conditioned self that made me obey others' directives, opinions, and expectations. I didn't know, I didn't see—because I wasn't present enough, because I wasn't integrated enough—that there are so many choices available to me in any given moment as I respect my needs and honor my intentions in a harmonious flow with others.

When I was later walking along Baghdad Boulevard, a famous thoroughfare on the Asian side of Istanbul, toward my friend's house, I felt a smile form on my face. Reflecting on those moments before I left home, I felt powerful. I felt present. Surprisingly, I also sensed warmth toward my mom and a deep connection with her. As I thought to myself, without her, how else could I have realized the individual freedom I've been seeking has been within me all along?

Describe the synchronicities you experienced when you got back in the flow: While I was walking, I remembered some of the cafés where I used to hang out with my friends back in the day. Numerous memories rushed into my head, filling me with nostalgia and joy. I texted a few of my friends to get together at one of these places again. Then I noticed a few shops that I wanted to go into. On the way back from visiting my friend, I looked around for some new shoes and bought a pair I'd been eyeing for some time. When I got back home, I was so high, I ran to my mom and gave her a big hug. I was filled with gratitude for her.

What is the inner feeling associated with the flow, and where do you feel it in your body? How does the physical sensation within your body create presence? I felt that gratitude in my chest. I intentionally spread it out of my heart into my palms, down to my feet, and up to the top of my head. I felt a bubble around my body—a strange sensation. I also felt inner freedom and power. I felt like I was walking on clouds, and even began to feel a little dizzy, until I reconnected with the earth through the bottoms of my feet. I enjoyed this high-conscious level of awareness, which eventually led me to grace and presence. I had such a lovely dinner that night with my family, feeling my deep love for my mom, and now—to my surprise—actually appreciating her controlling tendencies as she kept insisting that I eat more food. I smiled at her and took another scoop of lentil soup.

In the state of high-conscious presence, describe what kind of authentic self-expression or action intuitively comes to you as you honor the inner feelings that naturally arise: I realized how deeply connected I felt with my dad, my mom,

and my sister, Didem, that Christmas. I had
never felt such a natural flow with them until
that last visit, a few years ago. I took my walls
down. Without the need to defend my vulnerability, I took my mask off. I could now see their
conditioned selves very clearly, one by one: the
controlling one, the people pleaser, the perfectionist, the procrastinator. I then strangely realized that what I saw in them was exactly who
I was. Whatever repressed fears and hidden
desires I had, my family had probably experienced them too. After all these years, I suddenly
became aware that I'd been carrying a piece of
them with me. They were part of the Self that I'd
been working on my entire life. At that moment,
I came face-to-face with them. What I had been
running away from became my reflection. I saw
me in them, as they were in me.

You now hold the brush in your hands, standing in front of
an empty canvas, as the New Life appears in front of you. Start
painting! Create your own expression of your Self, the way you
feel it, the way your hands move, the way you follow your feet,
the way your brush dances with the colors of your own life
experiences. In order to keep your connection with higher levels of consciousness, keep moving through the doors of life to
relentlessly experiment with every moment you live. The New
Life, the New You, reflects a change in the way you see life,
how you respond to life, how you experience life. From here on,
every step you take represents the ever-increasing moments of
joy and fulfillment that are honest expressions of your Real
Self, the True One, the Pure One, who makes you rise and rise
until you realize your unyielding presence and your highest
potential—Ultimate Happiness.

GLOSSARY

(Terms are listed in the order that they were discussed in the book.)

Limiting Life Patterns

A repetitive cycle that starts and develops in your formative years when you're exposed to experiences that hurt you emotionally. Because you had neither the opportunity nor the ability to properly process the experience back then, you buried the emotional pain within your body. The System of Life has brought you back to similar life situations over and over again for you to process the original emotional hurt that you experienced in the first instance.

A typical limiting life pattern cycle runs as follows:

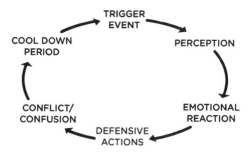

Trigger event is a person or situation that ignites an emotional reaction.

Perception is the lens you use to interpret a situation or a person's attitude or behavior.

Emotional reaction is the emotion that arises as a result of your perception when something or someone triggers you.

Defensive actions are the impulsive fight-or-flight actions intended to ward off the threat that a trigger represents. These actions take the form of aggressive, passive-aggressive, or passive behaviors that you deploy when triggered.

Conflict/Confusion is the state that you enter after your defensive actions, often resulting in arguments with others and/or inner doubts about your life decisions.

Cool down period is the period that follows the conflict and confusion phase of the limiting life pattern cycle, where everything said and done is forgotten or buried into the memory.

POWER Method

The method you use to break free from a limiting life pattern cycle, at the exact time of the trigger. It follows these steps:

PAUSE to notice and honor your emotions, as provoked by the trigger event.

OBSERVE your thoughts about the person or the situation that set off your emotional reactions.

WELCOME the physical sensations that your emotional reactions created in your body.

EARTH the physical sensations through three-by-three breath work, exhaling them out of your body, and discharging them into the earth through the bottoms of your feet.

RESPOND to the person or the situation by choosing your actions consciously and fully accepting whatever actions you take.

Three-by-Three Breath Work

A breath technique to loosen and discharge the physical sensations created in the body by the emotional response to a trigger. It involves a deep inhale into the physical sensation, followed by an exhale of the charge into the earth with a three-second hold between the breaths, repeated three times.

Self-Observation

The practice of creating a sense of space between you and your thoughts so you can take control of your awareness away from your subconscious and into your own hands. The self-observation meditation is how you practice getting hold of your attention whenever you are lost in your thoughts, in daydreaming.

Subconscious Internal Programming

The thought patterns, belief systems, and value sets that you form as a result of your past experiences to protect your vulnerability.

Repressed Fears

The fears that arose in the first incident that caused your emotional hurt and led you to avoid similar life experiences. Your repressed fears are your vulnerabilities, the sandbags you carry, and the root of suffering in life.

Hidden Desires

A survival mechanism that serves as an opposing force to your repressed fears, with the intention to hide your vulnerability from the outside world.

Thought Patterns

Overall mental constructs and conclusions you have formed based on your past life experiences to provide perspective. These patterns often repeat.

Belief Systems

Your convictions on how life should work, how people should behave, and how situations should happen.

Value Sets

Concepts you deem important and meaningful to you that you strive to live by.

Mind Value

A value driven by your subconscious internal programming, designed for survival.

Heart Value

A value driven by your true nature or essence, designed for joyful expression of Self.

Levels of Consciousness

Subconscious is the level of consciousness where the mind runs based on an automatic internal programming system, which in turn controls your instinctive fight-or-flight operating systems. These influence your perceptions, emotional reactions, and defensive actions.

Self-Conscious is the level of consciousness where the mind is self-aware and has the ability to observe and understand your subconscious internal programming. At this level, the mind can discern among different choices available as responses.

High-Conscious is the level of consciousness where the mind integrates your repressed fears and hidden desires to see reality objectively, thereby transcending your survival mechanisms and revealing the true nature and essence of your soul. This is where you will discover Ultimate Happiness.

Defensive Subconscious Strategies

You use the following three distinctive survival mechanisms to protect your vulnerability:

Defensive Actions are impulsive fight-or-flight actions intended to ward off a threat. They show up as aggressive, passive-aggressive, or passive behaviors that you deploy when triggered. For example, aggressive defensive actions may include yelling, hitting, or verbal or physical abuse, while passive-aggressive defensive actions may include complaining, gossiping, eye rolling, or giving the silent treatment. Passive defensive actions may include withdrawing, avoiding, leaving the room, or staying quiet.

Coping strategies are routine actions, such as addictions or obsessive-compulsive behaviors, that numb your emotional pain. Examples include excessive use of social media, TV, junk food, alcohol, cigarettes, sex, drugs, gambling, long hours of work, obsessive exercise, superstitious routines, and other excessive, repetitive, specific acts of comfort.

Conditioned Self is the mask you wear to hide your repressed fears and help you carry out your hidden

desires. For example, being a perfectionist is a conditioned self that hides the fear of not being good
enough, and being a high achiever is a conditioned self
that hides the fear of not being recognized.

Integration Process

The integration process takes place after identifying your
repressed fears and hidden desires, and their respective forces
in the body, to bring them together so you can process them at
the current level of your consciousness and ultimately rise to a
higher level of consciousness.

Three-by-Three Focus Work

This technique is used in the integration process to direct
the focus into the fists, and through the inner gaze and inner
awareness, to connect with each force and their respective
names. Focus is held in each fist for three seconds at a time
and alternates between the two fists for three cycles.

Assertive Self-Conscious Strategies

Doing the Opposite is a conscious response to a trigger in which you intentionally do something opposite from or different than how you usually react or
respond to a trigger.

Using I-Statements involves the conscious, matter-
of-fact expression of how you feel without expecting a
certain outcome.

Honoring Heart Values is the conscious pursuit of living in accordance with the values that best reflect your true nature and essence.

Integrative High-Conscious Strategies

Holding Space for Conscious Listening involves being present to listen consciously and with curiosity to give space to others for their true expressions of their own feelings.

Active Surrendering is the conscious release of control while retaining the ability to make changes or take charge while going with the flow.

Effortless Action stems from alignment among mind, heart, and body, which creates a powerful presence that moves you forward in the flow with more intention and integrity and with less effort and energy.

Living from Higher Integrity is a state of being where high-conscious feelings such as compassion, gratitude, forgiveness, joy, inspiration, inner knowing, grace, and presence naturally rise within you. It is from this place that you realize glimpses of Ultimate Happiness.

Self-Realization

The process of finding your Real Self through the journey of self-discovery.

Ultimate Happiness

An ultimate state of presence where you experience glimpses of life filled with joy, love, abundance, fulfillment, meaning, and purpose, and where you are fully aligned, integrated, and present.

ACKNOWLEDGMENTS

Writing a book is a personal, intimate, and vulnerable endeavor. It is a solitary activity, yet hardly a solo accomplishment.

This book is no longer an amateur manuscript because of G. Elizabeth Kretchmer's insightful guidance and expertise. I'm deeply thankful for her invaluable and encouraging comments—they made the book more intimate and personable, and the journey you are about to embark upon more magical.

I'm also deeply grateful to Dr. Gina Serraiocco for her early reviews of the manuscript and for providing helpful feedback on the flow and direction of the book. Her foreword also adds tremendous value as a professional testimonial to the message of this book.

Life is abundant. Life is resourceful. Life is the guide. I'm grateful to have met so many beautiful souls as fellow seekers, as clients, and as soulmates. Many intuitive healers and wise teachers and mentors have provided their divine guidance, and I'd like to offer them my sincere appreciation for their bright light, which has illuminated my path every step of the way.

Last, but not least, I'm grateful for my dad, Samih, and my mom, Güler, for being my loving parents, for bringing me to life, and for sharing their virtue and their humbleness. Without them I would have never been able to find my Real Self, and without them, this book would never have existed.

INSPIRATIONAL BOOKS
FOR FURTHER READING

Bourgeault, Cynthia. *The Holy Trinity and the Law of Three: Discovering the Radical Truth at the Heart of Christianity.* Boston: Shambhala, 2013.

Kriyananda, Swami. *The Essence of the Bhagavad Gita, Explained by Paramhansa Yogananda, As Remembered by His Disciple, Swami Kriyananda.* Crystal Clarity, 2006.

Meyer, Marvin, ed. *The Nag Hammadi Scriptures: The Revised and Updated Translation of Sacred Gnostic Texts.* HarperCollins, 2008.

Miller, Richard. *Yoga Nidra: A Meditative Practice for Deep Relaxation and Healing.* Sounds True, 2020.

Ouspensky, P. D. *In Search of the Miraculous: The Classic Exploration of Eastern Religious Thinking and Philosophy.* Harcourt, 1949.

Pagels, Elaine. *The Gnostic Gospels.* New York: Vintage Books, 1989.

Riso, Don Richard. *The Wisdom of the Enneagram: The Complete Guide to Psychological and Spiritual Growth for the Nine Personality Types.* New York: Bantam Books, 1999.

NOTES

1. Paul Reps and
   Nyogen Senzaki, Story 14, "Muddy Road," in *Zen Flesh, Zen Bones*, Kindle edition, 1998.
2. Bruce Lipton, *Biology of Belief: Unleashing the Power of Consciousness, Matter and Miracles* (Santa Rosa, CA: Mountain of Love/Elite Books, 2005), pp. 162–166.
3. Lisa Feldman Barrett, *How Emotions Are Made: The Secret Life of the Brain* (Boston: Houghton Mifflin Harcourt, 2017), from author's Ted@IBM talk in December 2017: "You Aren't at the Mercy of Your Emotions, Your Brain Creates Them."
4. Fleas in a jar experiment on YouTube: https://www.youtube.com/watch?v=v-Dn2KEjPuc.
5. "Writing 101: What Is the Hero's Journey? Two Hero's Journey Examples in Film," MasterClass, last updated Nov. 9, 2020, https://www.masterclass.com/articles/writing-101-what-is-the-heros-journey#joseph-campbell-and-the-heros-journey.
6. Plato, *The Republic*, Book VII, pp. 160–161, in Steven Cahn, ed., *Classics of Western Philosophy*, Seventh Edition (Indianapolis, IN: Hackett Publishing Company, Inc., 2006).
7. https://www.storynory.com/the-samurai-and-the-tea-master/.

ABOUT THE AUTHOR

 Arda Ozdemir is an executive life coach, spiritual mentor, qigong master, and the founder of Rise 2 Realize organization. He has helped thousands of people awaken to their fullest potential and experience ultimate happiness.

As a former finance executive in Silicon Valley, Arda embarked on his own personal transformation journey when he was looking to heal his chronic health issues, including depression and anxiety. His quest for cure led him to a series of explorations in wellness practices and ancient studies. This journey awakened him to his calling to guide others out of their suffering and emotional pain toward a life full of joy, fulfillment and meaning.

His teachings involve advanced self-empowerment methods using a combination of selected techniques from ancient and contemporary schools of spirituality, philosophy and psychology. With practicality and applicability in mind, he created the POWER method through perfecting his work with over 2,000 clients in the last 10 years. He offers this profoundly transformative method in fun, step-by-step workshops, mentorship programs, as well as in one-on-one sessions to individuals and couples.

Arda published his first book, *The Seeker's Manual*, in 2014, in which he described in detail the distinctive seven phases of a typical personal transformation journey.

www.rise2realize.com